English
National
Opera
Guide

4

Fidelio
Beethoven

English National Opera
receives financial
assistance from the Arts
Council of Great Britain
and the Greater London
Council.

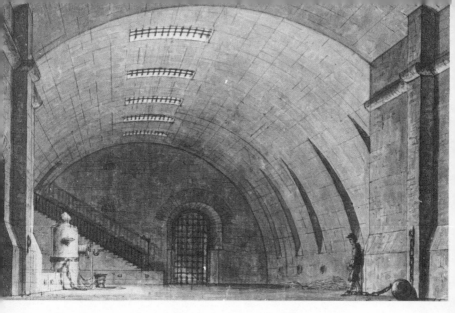

Nineteenth century set design for 'Fidelio' Act Two, scene one (Theater Museum, Munich)

Preface

English National Opera Guides are intended to be companions to opera in performance. They contain articles and illustrations relevant to any production and not only those mounted by English National Opera. Of general interest, also, is the inclusion of the complete original libretto of the opera, side by side with an English translation. There are many reasons why sung words may not be clearly distinguishable, whatever the language and however excellent the performance. The composer may have set several lines of text together, for instance, or he may have demanded an orchestral sound through which no voice can clearly articulate. ENO Guides supply English readers with an opportunity to know a libretto in advance and so greatly increase their understanding and enjoyment of performances whether live, broadcast or recorded.

ENO is very grateful to National Westminster Bank for sponsoring this *Fidelio* Guide, as well as a new production, in its wide ranging programme of community service. Such sponsorship is an indication of a steadily growing public interest in opera, and we hope the Guides will prove useful to new and experienced opera-lovers alike. An audience which knows what to look and listen for — one that demands a high standard of performance and recognises it when it is achieved — is our best support and, of course, an assurance for the future of opera in the English-speaking world.

Nicholas John
Editor

First published in Great Britain, 1980 by
John Calder (Publishers) Ltd.
18 Brewer Street
London W1R 4AS
and
in the U.S.A., 1980 by
Riverrun Press Inc.
Fifth Avenue,
New York 10016

4

Fidelio

Ludwig van Beethoven

English National Opera Guides Series Editor:
Nicholas John

This Guide is sponsored by
National Westminster Bank.

John Calder ● London
Riverrun Press ● New York

New York, NY 10010

ISBN 0 7145 3823   Paperback edition

BRITISH LIBRARY CATALOGUING DATA
Sonnleithner, Joseph Ferdinand
   Fidelio. — (English National Opera guides; 4).
   1. Operas — Librettos
   I. Title   II. John, Nicholas   III. Hammond, Tom
   IV. Blumer, Rodney   V. Beethoven, Ludwig van
   VI. Series
   782.1'2   ML50.B422

Typeset in Plantin by Alan Sutton Publishing Limited, Gloucester.
Printed by Whitstable Litho Limited in Great Britain.

Contents

List of Illustrations

Introduction

Elizabeth Forbes

Fidelio, because it is Beethoven's only opera, and because of the sublimity of the music and the nobility of its theme, has become a work unique in the operatic repertory, one to be approached with special reverence by audiences and performers alike. Yet Beethoven spent the last twenty years of his life searching for a suitable text for *Fidelio's* successor, while the opera itself was only one, and at the time by no means the most popular, of a category developed in France after the Revolution, and which spread to Italy, Germany and Austria — the 'Rescue' opera. Today, apart from *Fidelio* itself, the best known opera in this genre is Cherubini's *Les Deux Journées*, or *The Water Carrier* as it is usually called in English, which was first produced in Paris in January 1800. The text of *Les Deux Journées* was by Jean-Nicolas Bouilly, who two years previously had supplied the libretto for an opera by Pierre Gaveaux, performed at the Théâtre Feydeau, Paris, on February 19, 1798, and entitled *Léonore, ou l'amour conjugal*.

According to the author, this story of a wife who rescued her husband by dressing as a boy and taking a job in the prison where he was incarcerated, was based on an actual incident that took place during the Terror at Tours, where Bouilly then held an official position. He thought it prudent, in case of possible repercussions, to transfer the setting of the action from France to Spain. Two Italian versions of *Léonore*, much altered from the original, appeared during the next few years — Ferdinand Paer's *Eleonora ossia l'amore conjugale*, which was produced at Dresden in October 1804, and Simon Mayr's *L'amor conjugale*, first performed at Padua the following spring. In the latter work the setting was moved yet again, this time to Poland.

Meanwhile in Vienna the 34-year-old Beethoven had nearly finished composing a German version of the Bouilly libretto. Early in 1803 he had been engaged by Emanuel Schikaneder as resident composer at the recently opened Theater an der Wien, successor to the Theater auf den Wieden where *The Magic Flute* had first been performed a dozen years previously — a post which carried free accommodation in the theatre. The first rumours of an opera from Beethoven, the virtuoso pianist, were published in March. On April 5 he gave a concert in the Theater an der Wien whose programme included his First and Second Symphonies, the Piano Concerto in C Minor (No. 3) played by the composer himself, and the first performance of an oratorio, *Christ on The Mount of Olives*, which was criticised as being over-dramatic in style.

He was already suffering from the deafness that was to plague him for the rest of his life, becoming progressively worse year by year until the loss of hearing was complete. In his notebook for that year, among the preliminary sketches for his third symphony — the *Eroica* — is a trio for soprano, tenor and bass, the finale to an opera on the subject of Alexander the Great in India. This fragment probably represented an exercise in operatic writing, and was in any case not wasted, as will be seen. Then, in August, he was reported to be working on a libretto by Schikaneder — *Vestas Feuer* or *The Fire of Vesta* — but after composing some sketches for the first scene, he became disenchanted, both with the text and with its author. 'I have finally broken with Schikaneder', wrote Beethoven early in

7

January 1804, when returning a libretto on a theme 'connected with magic' to Johann Friedrich Rochlitz in Leipzig. 'Just picture to yourself a Roman subject (of which I had not been told either the scheme or anything else whatever) and language and verses such as could proceed only out of the mouths of Viennese *apple-women* — Well I have quickly had an old French libretto adapted and am now beginning to work on it'.

The 'old French libretto' was of course Bouilly's *Léonore*, translated and adapted by Joseph Sonnleithner, an official of the Vienna Court Theatres. At first Beethoven spoke hopefully of completing his opera by June 1804 but the following spring he had still not finished it. In the autumn he wrote to Sonnleithner, 'I am quite ready now — and am waiting for the last *four verses* — for which I have already thought out the theme provisionally — It is my *definite purpose* to write the overture during the rehearsals and not until then'. Sonnleithner kept close to Bouilly's original text but, by expanding the work from two to three acts, he fatally weakened its dramatic structure. Beethoven took immense trouble over his score; as his notebooks show, he rewrote the quartet in the first scene about a dozen times, and the aria for Florestan almost as frequently, while the theme of the trio-excerpt from the Alexander opera was used for the rapturous reunion between Leonora and Florestan in the latter's dungeon.

Fidelio, preceded by the overture now known as *Leonora No. 2*, was finally produced at the Theater an den Wien on November 20, 1805. Unfortunately for Beethoven and his opera, French troops had occupied Vienna exactly one week earlier, while Napoleon took up residence at the Palace of Schönbrunn two days after that. The inhabitants of the city were in no mood to give their attention to a new opera, not even — or more especially not — one devoted to the subject of freedom, and *Fidelio* was only repeated twice after the first performance, before being withdrawn.

Realising that the opera had failed chiefly because of the dramatic deficiencies of the libretto, and feeling strongly that so much wonderful music should not be allowed to disappear, Beethoven's friends urged him to revise his score. After a fiercely-fought, six-hour-long battle at the house of Prince Karl Lichnowsky, a patron of Beethoven's since the composer had first arrived in Vienna from Bonn, he agreed to make some cuts. The rearrangement of the three acts into two, and other alterations to the text, were made by Stephan von Breuning. Sonnleithner, perhaps luckily, was busy with the production of Cherubini's *Faniska*, an opera for which he had provided the libretto.

The revised *Fidelio* was given at the Theater an der Wien on March 29, 1806, preceded by a newly composed overture, *Leonora No. 3*. Beethoven was not at all pleased with the orchestral playing — 'the murdering of my music' as he put it — and after one more performance he quarrelled with Baron Peter von Braun (who had taken over the Theater an der Wien early in 1804) and withdrew his score. These first two versions of *Fidelio* are now generally entitled *Leonore*, as indeed the composer originally intended that they should be, though the theatre management at the time insisted on *Fidelio*, to avoid confusion with Paer's opera on the same subject.

During the next eight years Beethoven's thoughts were frequently turned towards opera. In October 1806, when the direction of the Court Theatres in Vienna passed into the hands of a group of noblemen, he applied for a permanent position as Court composer, offering to supply one opera and one lighter stage piece each year. His request was refused. Two years later he discussed the setting of *Macbeth* by Heinrich von Collin, author of the tragedy *Coriolan* for which Beethoven had composed an overture. He also briefly considered *Bradamante*, another work by the same writer. After Collin's death in 1811, Beethoven turned to Georg Friedrich Treitschke — of whom more will be heard — and toyed with the idea of a collaboration on *The Ruins of Babylon*. The following year he asked August von Kotzebue, for whose dramas *The Ruins of Athens* and *King Stephen*, specially written for the opening of the theatre in Pest, he had composed incidental music, to provide him with a libretto 'on a big historical subject, preferably from the Dark Ages, for example, about Attila . . .'. In 1813 he discussed *The Return of Ulysses* as a possible operatic theme with the poet Theodor Körner. Nothing came of any of these projects.

Then, in the New Year of 1814, three singers engaged at the Court theatre in Vienna, who were entitled to a benefit performance, broached the idea of a revival of *Fidelio* to its composer. Beethoven was by now an immensely distinguished figure in Viennese musical circles. His popularity had been augmented, late in 1813, by *Wellington's Victory*, or the Battle Symphony, which, originally conceived for performance in England, proved immensely successful in Vienna. The singers no doubt calculated that public interest in the opera, unheard for so long, would have greatly increased. There was, too, an excellent role in it for each of them. Johann Michael Vogl, the baritone who first interpreted so many of Schubert's songs, was to sing Pizarro, Karl Friedrich Weinmüller, a bass, would play Rocco and Herr Saal would take the part of Don Fernando. Beethoven had apparently mislaid his own score of *Fidelio*, and late in January or early in February he wrote to Count Moritz Lichnowsky (younger brother of his patron Prince Karl) to ask if he might borrow his copy. At the composer's

G F Treitschke in 1830 (1776 - 1842), lithograph by J. Kriehuber (Historisches Museum der Stadt Wien)

own request, the revision of the text, far more drastic than that of 1806 by Breuning, was to be undertaken by Treitschke, who was official poet as well as stage director at the Kärntnertor Theatre.

Treitschke's theatrical experience was backed by an innate sense of drama which ensured that this time Beethoven's opera would be thoroughly stageworthy. The composer's share of the revision was also more fundamental than before and every number in the score, apart from the March in the first act, underwent at least some musical rewriting. As usual, the work took much longer than Beethoven at first envisaged. There were also other distractions. He composed a song, *Germania*, for bass and chorus, to serve as finale to a *Singspiel* by Treitschke, *Die güte Nachtricht*, produced at the Kärntnertor Theatre on April 11, with Weinmüller as bass soloist. Before that, on February 27, he gave a concert in the Redoutensaal of the Hofburg, at which the Seventh Symphony, first performed the previous December, was repeated and the Eighth given its first performance.

'That accursed concert', complained Beethoven to Treitschke, 'has put me back in regard to the opera . . . Now, of course, everything has to be done at once and I could have composed something new far more quickly than patch up the old with something new, as I am now doing . . . Meanwhile the first act will be finished in a few days — But there is still much to be done to the second act and I have to compose a new overture as well . . . Before my concert I had just made a few sketches here and there — In short I assure you dear T., that this opera will win for me the martyr's crown. Had you not taken so much trouble with it and revised everything so satisfactorily, for which I shall ever be grateful to you, I would hardly bring myself to do my share — But by your work you have salvaged a few good bits of a ship that was wrecked and stranded'.

The stranded ship was relaunched on May 23, 1814 at the Kärntnertor Theatre. The new overture was not ready in time, and tradition has it that the overture to *The Ruins of Athens* was played instead. Treitschke himself says, in his memoirs, that the overture to the ballet *Prometheus* was used. A third alternative stems from Anton Schindler, who mentions 'an overture to *Leonore*', which could be construed as meaning the *Leonora No. 1*, thought by some, though not all, Beethoven scholars to have been composed for a projected performance of the second version at Prague in 1808 — a performance that did not materialise. At the second hearing of the third version, on May 25, 1814, the new overture, known ever since as the *Fidelio* overture, was definitely played.

One of the numbers cut in the 1806 revision of the opera had been the jailer Rocco's 'Gold' aria. At the seventh repeat of the third version, on July 18, 1814, which was a benefit performance for Beethoven, this aria, suitably revised by Treitschke and the composer, was reinstated for Weinmüller. There was also a new singer in the role of Pizarro. Vogl was ill and Beethoven gave the part to Anton Forti, a twenty-four-year-old bass whose voice, according to the composer, was better suited to the music than Vogl's. The change of cast meant extra rehearsals, of great advantage to the standard of performance.

In its new form, *Fidelio* was quickly taken up by theatres outside Vienna. Weber conducted the opera in Prague on November 27, 1814. The following year there were productions at Leipzig, Dresden and Berlin, where Leonora was sung at some of the performances by Anna Milder-

Anna Milder-Hauptmann (1785 - 1838), copper engraving by D. Weiss, from a drawing by Sigmund Perger. She created the role of Leonora at the age of nineteen in 1805. Haydn said, 'My dear girl, you have a voice the size of a house!'

Carolina Unger (Opera Rara Collection) and Henriette Sontag (Opera Rara Collection), two beautiful singers famous for their interpretations of his music. On one unfortunate visit to Beethoven, they drank some wine which did not agree with them and were both ill.

Hauptmann, the famous Austrian-born soprano who at the age of nineteen had created the role in the first (1805) version of the opera, at the Theater an der Wien. *Fidelio* reached St Petersburg in 1819, Amsterdam in 1824, Paris in 1829, London in 1832 and New York in 1839, by which time it had become one of the most popular and admired operas in the German repertory, a position which it has never subsequently lost. For the centenary of the first performance, in 1905, Richard Strauss conducted a revival of the original version at the Court Opera in Berlin, and the two hundredth anniversary of the composer's birth, in 1970, inspired other revivals of *Leonore*, including one by the Sadler's Wells Opera, as it then was, at the London Coliseum.

After the success of the third version of *Fidelio*, which Beethoven recognised was in large measure due to Treitschke, composer and poet planned

Wilhelmine Schröder-Devrient (1804 - 1860) in a pastel by E.B. Kietz (Beethoven-Haus, Bonn) and a lithograph by W. Santer (National Library, Vienna). She made her debut as Leonora in 1822 and became famous all over Europe for her interpretation of the part. Berlioz remembered how her arm shook from convulsive laughter as she stretched it out towards Pizarro.

Maria Malibran in the prison scene of 'Fidelio' in London 1836 (Theatre Museum)

an opera on the subject of Romulus and Remus. In January 1815, Beethoven wrote to Treitschke, 'I am composing *Romulus!* and shall begin to write it down one of these days'. But practical and financial difficulties intervened, and the following September he was complaining to his librettist that the Directors of the Court Opera were only willing to pay him the takings for one night for the proposed opera, 'and although I have so willingly offered, and still offer, many sacrifices to my art, yet by accepting such a condition I should lose far too much . . . I have asked the Theatrical Directors to pay me for *Romulus* 200 gold ducats and the takings for one night'.

The idea of an opera on the twin founders of Rome was not dropped for two or three years. Meanwhile, in January 1816, Beethoven wrote to Anna Milder-Hauptmann in Berlin to congratulate her. 'How I should like to be able to contribute in person to the enthusiasm of the Berliners which your performance in *Fidelio* has aroused . . . If you would ask Baron de la Motte Fouqué on my behalf to think out a subject for a grand opera which would also be suitable for *you*, then you would win great honour for me and for Germany's theatre. Moreover, I should like to set it to music solely for the *Berlin theatre*, for with these niggardly Directors in Vienna I shall never contrive to come to an arrangement for a new opera'. Nothing came of this idea either, and it is particularly ironic that Beethoven should have considered a collaboration with de la Motte Fouqué, as his last serious opera project was a poem by the distinguished poet and playwright Franz Grillparzer on the subject of *Melusine*. Grillparzer sent this libretto to Beethoven in 1823 but it had to be abandoned some three years later, because its theme was too close to that of *Undine*, the libretto which de la Motte Fouqué had adapted from his own story for E.T.A. Hoffmann's opera in 1816.

So *Fidelio* was destined to remain Beethoven's sole and glorious contribution to the operatic stage. When, in the aftermath of the Second World War, the many theatres in German-speaking countries destroyed by bombs, shells or fire re-opened their doors again, a large number of them did so with *Fidelio*, whose contemporary relevance was once more as vital and direct as in the years following the French Revolution. The extraordinary reception accorded to the work at the opening of the rebuilt Vienna State Opera in November 1955, a few weeks after the occupying powers had moved out of the city, bore witness to *Fidelio's* continuing and tremendous emotional impact.

'Fidelio': an operatic marriage

Basil Deane

Although Beethoven's early career as a composer was devoted above all to instrumental music, an artist with his innate dramatic sense was bound to be drawn to the stage. Moreover, success in the theatre was generally regarded as the pinnacle of achievement for a composer of the time. He was attracted by the most grandiose subjects from history and legend but in the event his only opera was based on an obscure incident that occurred within his own lifetime in provincial France. And for this the contemporary state of Viennese opera was largely responsible. By 1800 opera in Vienna was due for a renewal. The Italian forms of *opera seria* and *opera buffa* had outlived their attraction in the German-speaking capital. The German form of comic opera, the *Singspiel*, with its mixture of singing and spoken dialogue, its tendency towards exotic, magical or fantastic plots, had its limitations — limitations triumphantly transcended by Mozart in *The Magic Flute*, certainly. *The Magic Flute* was, however, inimitable and, in any case, Beethoven, much as he admired its high moral tone, was out of sympathy with its 'magical' elements. So the season of imported French opera, which took place in Vienna during 1803, was an eye-opener. Here, in such dramas as *Lodoïska* and *Les Deux Journées (The Water Carrier)* by Cherubini, Beethoven discovered an operatic path to follow. They were 'Rescue' operas, set, it is true, in some distant land or time but none the less relevant to the life and thought of the early 19th century. They exalted the ideals of marital love, of simple fidelity, of devoted heroism, and proclaimed the triumph of good over evil, of freedom over tyranny. Beethoven was overwhelmed. Ever afterwards Cherubini was for him the greatest of living composers, to be spoken of and listened to with deference. And he turned at once to the French writers in his search for a libretto. Bouilly was an obvious choice. He was a competent writer — indeed, his libretto for *The Water Carrier* was acknowledged by no less an authority than Goethe to be a masterpiece of its kind. But there were certain aspects of the French Revolutionary operatic libretto, arising out of its origins in the earlier 18th century *opéra comique*, that imposed restrictions and other problems for a composer attempting an elevated heroic style. The constant switch between spoken dialogue and music easily broke the musical continuity and the dramatic tension. Little provision was made for ensembles, or for extended finales. There was often an unresolved juxtaposition of the trivial and the portentous, the comic and the serious, the domestic and the stately. There was incident in plenty but little systematic working-out of dramatic relationships or character development. In short, the texts were primarily intended for musicians who were essentially short-winded and undemanding. And if these descriptions were inappropriate to the best French composers, such as Cherubini and Méhul, they certainly did not apply to Beethoven. So *Fidelio* is the offspring of the union of two very different artistic worlds: those of the French librettist and the German composer, of literary naivety and musical profundity, of nearsightedness and far-ranging vision. What the two artists shared, and what ultimately makes for the supreme greatness of the opera, is a common idealism, a belief in the essential goodness of man, a conviction that right, in the end, will triumph. Yet the birth was not an easy one, as Beethoven

15

confessed to Schindler: 'Of all the children of my spirit, this one is dearest to me, because it was the most difficult to bring into the world'. The story of Beethoven's travails, and of the contributions made by his three Viennese librettists to the adaptation of the text, is a fascinating one. But here we shall look at the final revision of 1814, which is, of course, the form in which the work is most commonly presented.

Overture

Beethoven's problems began with the overture. Theorists of his day were much exercised by the role and nature of the overture to an opera. Should it prepare the spectators for the opening scene? Or should it rather foreshadow the end of the opera? Should it express the range of emotions to be experienced in the course of the drama? Should it even (as one writer suggested) attempt to indicate the earlier events leading up to the forthcoming action? Should it use themes from the opera, or not? There was no common consensus. But French composers sometimes anticipated later themes in their overtures, and the story of the three versions of the *Leonora* overture is the story of Beethoven's attempt to reconcile thematic reference, and the formal freedom of the French musicians, with his own superb sense of musical structure. Although *Leonora No. 3* is the most complete and satisfying version, it *does* anticipate the whole course of action and on that account is, in purely dramatic terms, unsuitable as a curtain raiser. (The custom of playing it in the course of the opera is open to the same objection.) So, however much we may justly admire the earlier overtures, the *Fidelio* overture undoubtedly makes the most suitable prelude to the opera. It is formally coherent, and dramatic, without pre-empting the ensuing action. Two of the principal sentiments of the work, heroic energy and romantic tenderness, are adumbrated in the opening bars of the introduction, as the confidently rising fanfare is answered by a soft horn call [1]. On its second appearance the horn call takes us into mysterious harmonic regions, but a crescendo and an insistent drum stroke compel a return in preparation for the Allegro. Here the main theme derives its initial shape from the fanfare, and its colour from the horn. The vigorous exposition is followed by a quiet, delicately shaded passage, in which the woodwind play with the main theme. This leads unobtrusively into the recapitulation, which in turn reintroduces the opening bars of the overture. The horn call is now enhanced with triplet arabesques of Schubertian grace. But a final Presto, taking up the dotted rhythm and adding the weight of the trombones to the orchestral forces, concludes the overture on a burst of jubilant energy.

Act One

No.1 Duet: MARCELLINA, JACQUINO

The opening scene of the opera presents a domestic situation of the type frequently encountered in French opera at the time. It is set in the courtyard of a state prison, not far from Seville. In the first two versions of the opera the action started with Marcellina's solo, now No.2, with the duet placed second. By reversing this order in the later version, Beethoven begins with the A major duet, which follows appropriately on the E major of the overture. Marcellina, the daughter of the jailer, Rocco, is engaged in her domestic duties. Jacquino, the porter, is attempting to propose to her, despite repeated interruptions from callers at the gate. She deftly evades his

Elizabeth Schwarzkopf (Marcellina) and Dennis Stephenson (Jacquino) at Covent Garden in 1948 (photo: Edward Mandinian; by courtesy of the Archives of the Royal Opera House)

importunate questioning and, when his back is turned, expresses her love for Fidelio, her father's young assistant. The music contrasts Jacquino's impatience with Marcellina's daydreaming. The opening motive [2], with its concise rhythmic shape, reappears in various guises, and Jacquino's first phrase [3] epitomises both the general Mozartian style and, in the rather angular triplets of the third bar, Beethoven's individual touch.

Jacquino, increasingly frustrated, is called away by Rocco, and Marcellina, at last able to relax, turns her thoughts again to Fidelio. She thinks he is well disposed to her, but what of her father?

No.2 Aria: MARCELLINA

Marcellina is essentially a simple soul, and her one aria defines her personality. As her thoughts develop from almost timid reflection upon her present situation of undeclared love to hope of future bliss, so the music changes from a hesitant minor to a confident major, the major section itself being a variation of the preceding one [4 and 5]. The orchestral accompaniment underlines the change, and its palpitations foreshadow Florestan's great aria. Although the vocal line remains the same in each of the two verses, Beethoven embellishes the accompaniment in the second, and concludes the aria with a characteristically bright C major coda.

Rocco, followed by Jacquino, appears, and asks if Fidelio has not returned with dispatches for the Governor. The disguised Leonora arrives, laden with chains and provisions. Rocco praises his assistant's economical purchasing, and promises a reward, hinting that he can see into Fidelio's heart.

No.3 Quartet: MARCELLINA, LEONORA, JACQUINO, ROCCO

Up until this point in the action Beethoven and his collaborators kept closely to the French libretto, and consequently the implied range of the drama hardly exceeds that of an 18th century domestic comedy. Now the opera takes on a wholly new dimension. There is no precedent in Bouilly's text for the quartet, which was included in the work from the first version onwards. No doubt Beethoven and his original librettist, Sonnleithner, felt the need to expand Bouilly's framework by introducing an element which would further define the relationships of the characters already presented, and would at the same time provide a concerted number of substantial proportions at this point in the opera. All four characters react to the situation in different ways. Marcellina is delighted; Leonora is apprehensive; Jacquino is jealous; Rocco is benevolent. Yet Beethoven, paradoxically, chooses for his setting the musical form that, above all others, seems to preclude differentiation of emotion — the canon, in which each voice in turn follows faithfully the course of its predecessor. It is the mark of his supreme genius that the pathos of this situation is enriched, not diminished, by his adherence to the strict form. And this is because the sheer beauty and tenderness of the music gives an emotional depth to the movement which embraces all the individual reactions. Here, for the first time in the opera, Leonora herself is presented in music. And it is *her* love, *her* nobility, the root causes of the deception which has, in spite of herself, led to this situation, that determine the musical essence of the quartet, in the quiet string harmonies of the introduction [6] and the ensuing melodic phrase [7]. The subtlety of colouring in the orchestral accompaniment looks forward to the music of the composer's last period. In the final version of the opera Beethoven shortened the musical numbers in almost every case: the quartet remained virtually unaltered.

Rocco promises to speed the betrothal, but warns that something besides love is essential for domestic contentment . . .

No.4 Aria: ROCCO

. . . Gold. Gold brings love and authority. It fulfils desires, and invites the benevolence of Fortune. Rocco is portrayed as a bluff, forthright

character with a keen sense of financial advantage, as his earlier appro-
bation of Fidelio showed. With this return to the original source, we are
brought back again to the realms of comic opera, and the aria belongs to a
familiar *buffo* type, with alternating sections, contrasted in tempo and
metre [8 and 9]. In his first version of the aria Beethoven included
trumpets and drums. His later decision to reduce the scoring gives Rocco a
less bombastic appearance.

Leonora is torn by conflicting impulses. The talk of a marriage is
inevitably distressing. She is, however, dependent on Rocco's continued
goodwill to gain access to the prisoners and to seek out her husband. She
temporises. She acknowledges that the union of two loving hearts is the
source of true happiness but, in addition, she needs something else — his
trust. She presses the point, and begs to be allowed to assist him with his
duties among the prisoners. Rocco is persuaded to ask the Governor's
permission to allow Fidelio to go with him into the dungeons — although
there is one dungeon where she may never penetrate. The prisoner has
been immured there for over two years. Leonora reacts at once. 'Two
years? He must be a dangerous criminal'. 'Or he must have dangerous
enemies', Rocco replies. The prisoner's rations, on the orders of the
Governor, are being reduced to starvation level, and he will soon die. He
has neither light, nor straw bedding. Marcellina begs her father not to let
Fidelio see this distressing sight. Leonora, flaring up, exclaims, 'Why not?
I have strength, and courage'.

No.5 Trio: MARCELLINA, LEONORA, ROCCO

Now the opera abruptly moves on to a new plane of dramatic intensity,
one that it is not to leave before the final resolution. The 'domestic' action
involving the relationship of Marcellina and Jacquino becomes irrelevant.
From the preceding dialogue Leonora derives both hope and fear. She
believes she may have found her husband. Yet if so, he is in deadly danger,
and only she can save him. She is a prey to various emotions. She is
resolute, and will pay whatever price is demanded. She prays that hope will
bring release from her bitter tears. The comforting sentiments of her two
companions, who are of course ignorant of her true situation, merely
underline her predicament. The emotional tension is established by the
staccato strings and stabbing chords of the opening. There are certain key
words in the opera, here as elsewhere, which evoke a graphic response from
the composer. Leonora's comparison of love (Liebe) and sorrows (Leiden)
provokes a sudden switch from major to minor, and a florid elaboration of
the phrase [10]. The reference to the healing power of hope is set to a
phrase of melting tenderness [11]. And tears — bitter for Leonora, sweet
for Marcellina — inspire a poignant falling motive [12], followed by a chain
of descending thirds. All this detail takes its place in the overall sweep of
the music. The two hundred bars of the trio establish a new musical
dimension in the opera, and indeed the ensemble served as the Finale of
the first act in Beethoven's original version.

Rocco announces that he will ask the Governor for his consent to the
projected marriage, and to the proposal that Fidelio should have access to
all the prisoners. Distant music is heard.

No.6 March

During the march, which, despite its brevity, is one of Beethoven's most attractive essays in the genre, the Governor, Don Pizarro, enters with his retinue. He issues some orders, takes his dispatches, and opens a letter, which he reads aloud after dismissing the prison staff (Leonora, however, contrives to remain). Pizarro is warned by the writer that the Minister has heard that some prisoners are being unlawfully detained, and intends to pay a surprise visit the next day. He reflects that the discovery of Florestan in chains would ruin him; but he sees a way out — one bold deed will settle the matter.

No.7 Aria with Chorus: PIZARRO

The treatment of Pizarro underlines the gulf between Beethoven and his sources. He is of course central to the drama, yet in Bouilly's libretto Pizarro was a spoken role, a situation which deprived any intending composer of a major musical dimension, as Beethoven and Sonnleithner realised.

The villain in early 19th century drama is an unqualified one, and Beethoven had no occasion to modify the depth of his dye. But mere parody would not be enough. Pizarro *is* a real man of flesh-and-blood, a terrifying figure in a context of absolute power. As this century has cause to know, the most fearful tyrant is the psychopath whose vindictiveness is thinly disguised, whose self-control is fragile, whose outbursts are unpredictable. Thus Pizarro. His inner agitation is expressed, in the time honoured way, by the orchestra: the ominous drum roll; the twisting string figure [13], which seems like a perversion of Leonora's 'tear' motive [12]; the stabbing accents; the blaring brass. His own line begins with the angular interval of B flat — C sharp [14], and it is characterized throughout by short phrases whose irregular outlines and leaps seem to be intent on breaking the bounds of normal musical restraint. The transition from minor to major as he gloats in anticipation of his revenge is a travesty of the meaning the progression generally conveys in Beethoven's music. And the cowed murmurings of the chorus serve to emphasise his invulnerability.

After the aria Pizarro commands, with appropriate threats, that a watch shall be kept, and a trumpet sounded when any escorted carriage shall be seen approaching from Seville. Then he summons Rocco.

No.8 Duet: PIZARRO, ROCCO

Pizarro needs Rocco's complicity, in order to carry out his design. He begins, shrewdly enough, by attacking the jailer's weak point, and promises to make him rich. He flatters Rocco by praising his courage, developed through long service, before revealing to his impatient servant what the jailer must do — 'Murder'. The word is given its full horror by the *mezza voce* drop in pitch [15]. Rocco, aghast, can only stammer at first, then pulls himself together, and points out that murder is not part of his statutory duties. Pizarro, no doubt anticipating this refusal, undertakes to do the deed himself and identifies his victim as the dying prisoner. Rocco's task is merely to dig the grave. Rocco, relieved, eases his conscience by reflecting that the poor man would in any case be better off dead. The continuity of the music is unbroken by the recitative in which Pizarro announces the detail of his plan.

No.9 *Recitative and Aria:* LEONORA

Leonora, now left alone, is deeply suspicious of Pizarro's intentions. She expresses her horror at his cruelty but hope consoles her and she renews

Gwyneth Jones as Leonora at Covent Garden (photo: Alfredo Evan; by courtesy of the Archives of the Royal Opera House)

her determination to follow the course, strengthened by the devotion of true married love. Although in his final version Beethoven shortened the aria, he entirely rewrote the recitative, greatly increasing its importance. In its colour, its dramatic changes of mood from anger to tenderness, it belongs to Beethoven's full maturity. The aria itself takes its character from its unusual scoring for strings and obligato accompaniment of three horns and bassoon. The voice begins with one of Beethoven's most serenely beautiful melodies [16] and flowers into delicate ornamentation, entwining with the accompanying instruments. In the concluding quick section, wide-ranging agility on the part of singer and instrumentalists expresses Leonora's fixity of purpose.

Marcellina and Jacquino return, still quarrelling about Fidelio. Leonora, anxious to inspect the prisoners, begs Rocco to allow them out into the courtyard. He gives permission but, to her disappointment, only for the prisoners in the upper cells.

The treatment of this incident illustrates the tightening of the dramatic motivation by successive librettists. In the French original, which Sonnleithner followed, the prisoners are allowed a daily exercise period, and Marcellina releases them on the orders of the Governor. Breuning devolved this action to Leonora. Treitschke went further, and attributed their release to an act of grace in defiance of the Governor, instigated by Leonora herself.

21

The prisoners' chorus at Her Majesty's Theatre, 1851 (BBC Hulton Picture Library)

No.10 Finale Act One

Leonora and Jacquino unbar the prisoners' doors, and one by one the captives emerge into the sunlight, against a quiet string texture, which expands and then contracts again. This shape foreshadows the ensuing scene. The prisoners begin their chorus hesitantly, as they breathe in the life-giving air, and compare it to the grave-like dungeons [17]. The key changes from B flat to a bright G major, and one of them steps forward and proclaims that with God's help they will find once again freedom and peace — the rest respond with an outburst of joy [18]. Then they realise that they are overheard by the guards, and they take up the opening chorus, this time in a whisper, and fall silent. No moment in opera is more profoundly moving, none has more universal meaning than the emergence of these anonymous prisoners from darkness into light.

Rocco returns from an interview with the Governor, and tells Leonora that his two requests have been granted, and that she may accompany him into the dungeons this very day. She is at first delighted, then dismayed to learn that their task is to dig a grave for the Governor's victim. With ominous solemnity Rocco describes where they shall dig the grave [19]. He would like to spare her the unpleasant duty but, apprehensive though she now is, she insists on going with the jailer.

Jacquino and Marcellina arrive, breathless, with dramatic news. The Governor has heard that the prisoners have been allowed out and is in a fury [20]. Pizarro himself appears and rages at Rocco, demanding to know why he disobeyed orders [21]. Rocco, after the initial shock, recovers his composure and placates his master, by saying that it is the King's name day, and that moreover a death will soon take place. The prisoners, their hopes of freedom dashed, are shepherded back to their cells, bidding a lingering farewell to the light of day [22], while Pizarro urges Rocco to hasten to his grisly task.

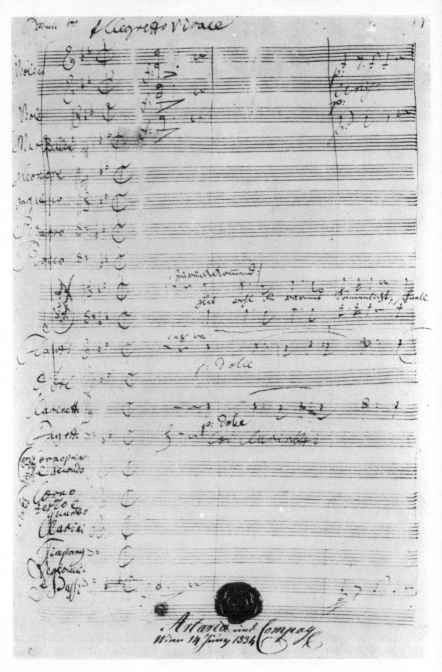

The autograph score of 'Leb wohl, du warmes Sonnenlicht' (Bildarchiv Preussischer Kulturbesitz, Berlin)

Julius Patzak as Florestan at the 1949 Salzburg Festival. His performance is described by Lord Harewood in 'Opera on Record' as of extraordinary quality — 'the uncannily evocative diction, the sensitive, even serene vocal line, the constant intensity' (photo: Ernst Hausknost)

Act Two

No.11 Introduction and Aria: FLORESTAN

The orchestral introduction in F minor sets a mood of sombre foreboding. It is a masterpiece of orchestral colouring, in which each section of the orchestra plays a distinctive part in the texture — not the least remarkable is that of the drums, tuned, most unusually, to A and E flat, a diminished fifth, the interval which medieval musicians regarded as 'diabolical'. A momentary gleam of light after a major cadence is overwhelmed by the prevailing gloom. And, in this respect, the music matches the scene revealed by the rising curtain — Florestan's dungeon, illumined only by a flicker of light. From the desolate figure comes a great cry, 'God! what darkness here!' [23]. Nothing else lives in the solitude. But God's will is best, and His the reckoning. The remarkable harmonies supporting the recitative [24] lead into the A flat aria, whose theme, announced by clarinets, bassoons and horns, appears in each of the Leonora overtures [25]. In music whose expressive beauty equals that of Leonora's aria, Florestan reflects on his unjust fate and finds consolation in the knowledge that he has done his duty. Then he rises in ecstasy as he sees a vision of his beloved wife Leonora leading him to freedom [26]. The vision fades, he sinks back exhausted, and the music dies away. This F major section, with its oboe obbligato, was written for the final version of the opera, and provides a much more dramatically effective conclusion to the scene than did the earlier F minor section it replaced.

No.12 Melodrama and Duet: LEONORA, ROCCO

Rocco and Leonora enter Florestan's dungeon. Leonora tries in vain to discern the prisoner's features before they begin their task of preparing the grave. Melodrama, the declamation of speech against an instrumental background, was a familiar feature of contemporary French opera, applied at moments of high dramatic tension in the dialogue. Beethoven uses it effectively here to create the atmosphere for the following duet, directed to be performed softly throughout. It is a remarkably evocative piece. The quietly repeated chords on low muted strings and woodwind create a sense of urgency, while the rumbling figure in the bass [27] imbues the music with sinister meaning. The dialogue between the two protagonists is hushed and to the point, until Leonora, distracted by her thoughts of Florestan, allows her attention to wander, and is recalled to her duties by Rocco.

Florestan awakes, and is recognised by Leonora, who, despite her overwhelming emotions, must continue to conceal her identity. He learns that he has been imprisoned by Don Pizarro, whose crimes he exposed. He asks for a drink, and Leonora gives him some wine.

No.13 Trio: LEONORA, FLORESTAN, ROCCO

Florestan expresses his gratitude in music of lyrical warmth [28], and the others respond. Leonora persuades the reluctant Rocco to allow her to give the starving prisoner a piece of bread she is carrying in her pocket. The opening phrase returns, and Florestan again thanks his unknown benefactor. Leonora finds the situation more than she can bear, and Rocco reflects that the prisoner will soon be dead.

Pizarro enters, intent on accomplishing his purpose, and draws a dagger.

No.14 *Quartet:* LEONORA, FLORESTAN, PIZARRO, ROCCO

Against a turbulent orchestral background Pizarro gloats over his victim. He reveals his identity in a phrase of characteristically chromatic outline [29]. Then the chromaticism gives place to a triumphant D major as he moves to the kill. He is prevented by Leonora, whose turn it now is to

*Lotte Lehmann
as Leonora*

disclose her own identity, in an utterance of soaring defiance, 'First kill his wife!' [30]. Pizarro renews his attempt on Florestan, but is halted by a trumpet call from the tower [31]. There is a moment of stunned silence as the protagonists register the significance of the interruption, and then follows a phrase of ethereal calm, incorporated also into the third Leonora overture [32]. The trumpet sounds again. Jacquino announces the arrival of the Minister, and the quartet ends in a tumult of excitement. Pizarro rushes out, the others leave, and Leonora and Florestan are left alone.

In the earlier versions, the lovers were still in suspense as to their ultimate Fate. Would Rocco cover up for his master? But in the final revision, the clouds are lifted. Rocco demonstrates his goodwill to them before following Pizarro. Leonora reassures Florestan that all will be well.

No.15 Duet: LEONORA, FLORESTAN

Throughout the opera the love between Leonora and Florestan has been the mainspring of the action. Now it is expressed in music of ecstatic happiness. All the frustrations and terrors of separation and the unknown are resolved in this brilliant, surging G major duet [33].

One of Rex Whistler's designs for 'Fidelio' at Covent Garden in 1934 (photo: Edward Mandinian; by courtesy of the Archives of the Royal Opera House)

No.16 Finale

The scene is the parade ground of the castle. The Minister, Don Fernando, is surrounded by his officers. Pizarro is also present. Jacquino and Marcellina lead in the prisoners. The introduction takes the form of one of Beethoven's massive crescendos on tonic and dominant, in the triumphal key of C major. The crowd burst into jubilation. Don Fernando, in broad stately phrases [34], proclaims the King's dedication to justice for all. Rocco produces Leonora, and Florestan, still in chains. Their case is explained to the astonished Minister by Rocco. The crowd demand that Pizarro should be punished, and he is taken away by the guards. Don Fernando invites Leonora to remove Florestan's fetters. Here the mood changes, as Beethoven introduces into his score an extract from his early *Cantata on the Death of Joseph II*. In the cantata Joseph is praised for having overcome Fanaticism, a monster from Hell who spread darkness

27

over the earth. The music is taken from the aria, 'Mankind rose up to the light, and the sun warmed the earth with the rays of the Godhead.' The parallelism is clear, and this F major section with its beautiful melodic curve [35] provides a moment of general reflection on the mystery of God's mercy and justice. Then all is celebration as the chorus lead off with a line from Schiller's *Ode to Joy* : 'Let him who has won a fair wife join in our rejoicing'.

Death is swallowed up in victory; captivity is led captive; the light shines in the darkness; love conquers all. 'Music' declared Beethoven, 'is a higher revelation than all your wisdom and philosophy.' As the curtain comes down on *Fidelio*, who will be the first to contradict him?

An extract from 'Beethoven the Creator'

Romain Rolland
translated by Ernest Newman

Romain Rolland's study of 'Beethoven, Les Grandes époques créatrices' was published in French between 1928 and 1957. The first volume entitled 'De l'Héroïque à l'Apassionata' (1928) contains a chapter devoted to 'Leonore'. Since the whole work is at present out of print in Britain, an extract from Newman's translation is given here as a short example of this remarkable piece of critical appreciation.

What then is this work that kept its place in Beethoven's affections until the last, and of which three successive versions and four (if not five) overtures were insufficient to satisfy his *Sehnsucht*, his passionate desire to realise it? Note the fact that the overtures, with the exception of the fourth, are not simply introductions to the work but separate and independent attempts at the solution of the same problem, fresh desperate efforts to convey the idea of the work by purely symphonic means! Why this pertinacity? Did he see a dramatic-musical problem to resolve? Assuredly, as we shall see, Beethoven brought into the opera house a new form, and his instinct must have made him aware of its difficulties and of the insufficiency of certain realisations of it. But would it not have been simpler, and more consonant with his nature, that took more pleasure in inventing than in re-touching, to approach the problem afresh in a new work instead of obstinately working again and again over the old one? What was there in this work that bound him to it so? What was the unique nature of it? Was it perhaps the subject?

Before examining it more closely, one detail ought to put us on our guard. At the end of the libretto, — which is virtually a translation from the French — Beethoven introduces into the final chorus — *maestoso* for four voices, then *tutti* — these words of Schiller:—

'*Wer ein holdes Weib errungen, stimm' in unseren Jubel ein!*' ('Let him who has won him a dear wife, join us in our joy!')

Twenty years later he will use these same words again in the hymn to Joy at the end of the Ninth Symphony, so much did the thought mean for him!

That life-long dream of his, that it was never given to him to realise! That idealisation of women and of conjugal fidelity, in which, in spite of all deceptions, he has never ceased to believe! I am not speaking now of the refusals he received, but of the bitter revelations life brought him with regard to the women he had loved, and that made him say to Nanni Giannatasio del Rio in 1817:—

'I have never known a marriage in which, after a time, one or other of the pair has not regretted the false step. And of the few women the possession of whom would formerly have seemed to me supreme happiness, I have lived to see that it was a good thing that not one of them became my wife. Ah! How fortunate it is that often the vows of mortals are not accomplished!'

No matter! He is never an apostate to his religious ideal of the betrothed, the wife. He will render her in public a solemn homage, in his two greatest works, the one dramatic, the other choral.

In the same way Goethe, who no doubt had less apparent reason to think himself unfortunate in love, but who, in reality, having known it better had also more reason to know its insufficiency and its bitterness, Goethe, who could not find or keep a companion worthy of him, cannot make his exit from life before he has sung, in the Epilogue to *Faust* his credo in woman.

Possibly thoughts of this kind seem, to our aesthetes of to-day, to lie outside the circle of art. But since the emperor of art, Goethe, has sealed his greatest work with them, I have some right to note their secret importance in the mind of Beethoven, and the part they played in the enduring attraction that the theme of *Fidelio* had for him.

☆

Let us return to this theme.

It has been much disparaged. The general opinion rather looks down on it, and the wretched performances the work has had during a whole century have confirmed this verdict. It must be confessed that until our time *Fidelio* was played in a way that misrepresented it.

Let us study it more closely. Anyone who has had the good fortune, as I had, to see the centenary performances at Vienna must make his *mea culpa* for the misunderstanding of a century; and one feels the need to share the discovery with others, — the newly-revealed splendour, dramatic and musical, of the entire second act, that unique masterpiece that had no forerunner and has had no successor in the musical theatre. And without a shadow of doubt the grandeur of it is wholly the work of the genius of the musician. Yet the poem has not served him ill; this libretto is a sturdy horse that does not stumble under the weight of its rider. Beethoven did it justice: he maintained *mordicus* that the subject was an excellent one. In 1823, when he was chatting with Weber and joking about the libretti of his younger colleague, and expressing himself scathingly on the incurable mediocrity of the German librettists, he paid the French a compliment and recalled the fact that his *Fidelio* came to him from them.

☆

What came to him from them, in *Leonora*, was not merely an anecdote more or less well told but an atmosphere of tragic reality: it was the Revolution.

But the French themselves, — as happens to those who, absorbed in an event, their nose to the detail of the daily round, cannot see the great eternal lines — had been unconscious of the Æschylean breath that came from their tale. Just as in the *Eroica* Beethoven had been the Homer of the Empire, so now, in *Leonora*, he was the Æschylus of the Revolution.

Everyone knows the story of *Leonora* is taken from Bouilly, who himself was not its inventor, for he had known the heroine of it — a woman of Touraine. He has given an account of her in his memoirs; but Beethoven knew nothing of these, for they did not appear until after his death; and *Leonora* came to him in the Spanish costume in which Bouilly, for prudential reasons, had disguised it. There is no Spanish local colour in his music, however; and his intuition, that pierces to the eternal depths, seems to have divined the proximity of the terrible period he was describing — at no more than ten years' distance from the real drama, and when the actual heroine was still alive.

There is no need for me to tell again the story of the drama, which, in its broad lines, depicts the horrors of a State prison and the devotion of a woman who entered it in diguise to save her husband. The critics have in general insisted only on the improbabilities and incongruities of the libretto, or on the difficulty that Beethoven's symphonic genius had in adapting itself to the dramatic necessities of opera. We are entitled to assume that they have not perceived the true essence either of the poem that Beethoven was setting or of the dramatic Ode he wished to make of it.

To the first of these points some effective answers have recently been made. Hermann W. von Waltershausen* has undertaken the defence of the French libretto. He shows that the mixture of styles, that has been so freely criticised — the bourgeois opening that hardly prepares us for the high tragedy that is to come — comes from a view of the subject that is as veracious as it is striking. At the height of the Terror, even in the darkness of this prison in which, it would seem, those who have entered have left all hope behind, the tranquil life of the bourgeois goes on just the same, with its pots of geranium in the window, the young girl's love-dreams, the old gaoler's simple and affectionate calculations of self-interest, his quiproquos and his comic vexations. But the art is in the lightness of the touches, in the imperceptible oncoming of the tragic shadow, that at first just touches these scenes of egoistic tranquillity with the tip of its wing, then reaches further, and at last envelops the whole stage. The French librettist has indicated this. It is not without interest for us that these *poetae minores* (the word poet is a big one!) of the French bourgeois comedy and opéra-comique did much, according to the German historians, to form that atmosphere of chiaroscuro and mysterious terror in which German musical romanticism found its nourishment. From these *crescendi* of inexplicable anguish and terror, Weber, in *Der Freischütz*, drew effects till then unknown. Our poor French librettists were far enough from these; no doubt these agitations would have frightened them; they had undergone too many of them in the life of the time not to tone them down in their comedies. In the same way some of our writers of to-day who witnessed and were wounded in the bloody catastrophe of the Europe they knew, fly from the representation of it in their art; but in spite of them their aesthetic diversions bear the agitated imprint of it. The obscure source of the tragic perturbation that was so much to the liking of romanticism was the social agitation, — the terror during the Terror — of the preceding generation. What that generation had been able only to stammer forth, a Beethoven expresses in its naked truth, without any beating about the bush, out of the plenitude of a great heart and with the mastery of genius. His *Leonora* is a monument of the anguish of the period, of the oppressed soul and its appeal to liberty, — a formidable *crescendo* swelling from suffering to joy, traversing the road of hope and combat — an ascent from the abyss to the clear sky.

This filiation between a robust junior and the elder members of a noble race — these, however, a trifle debilitated and overborne by the rigours of the time, — is not confined merely to vague moral resemblances. It is clearly marked in the music, with a precision that permits of no doubt. The symphonic style of *Leonora* derives in essentials from that of Méhul and Cherubini. Here again it has been able to ripen the rather green and dry

* Neues Beethoven —— Jahrbuch, 1924: zur Dramaturgie des *Fidelio*

fruit, to press out the whole of the juice of it where they were content with a few drops.

We have to remember that in the *Leonora* period Beethoven, who could still hear, enjoyed the French operas that were the delight of Vienna; and for him no living master could compare with Cherubini. Among the *Fidelio* sketches we find, in Beethoven's writing, passages from *The Water Carrier*. Seyfried and Schindler bear testimony to his unceasing admiration for the composer of *Medea*; and we know that Beethoven himself, at the height of his genius (in 1823), wrote to Cherubini paying humble homage to this work.

It is not surprising, then, that traces of this influence should be found in his own music. Even during his lifetime E.T.A. Hoffmann, who always saw more deeply than his contemporaries, had been struck by the community of race between Cherubini's overtures and the *Coriolan*. Since that time Wagner and the German critics of our own day have pointed out several resemblances between them. The question has recently been elucidated, so far as the Beethoven overtures are concerned, by Arnold Schmitz (1925).* The examples he gives, the similarities he notes, show clearly that Beethoven derived a good deal from the French composers of the Revolution; but they prove also the magnificent use he made of his booty. If some of the analogues may be explained on the theory of a common source — Gluck (for example, the mighty unisons with which all Beethoven's tragic overtures open) — the majority of the others bear witness to the moral contagion of the France that has as yet barely emerged from the Revolution and still felt the shock of it; a whole family of characteristic effects or motives in the operas of Méhul and Cherubini exhibits the nervous fever, the uneasy agitation, the painful excess of excitement of which I spoke a moment ago in connection with the poems; the composers may not have been clearly conscious of it, but for long enough afterwards it ran shuddering beneath their skin, like the periodic attacks of an old malaria. Schmitz has drawn up a remarkable inventory of them: the obstinate use of certain stereotyped formulae for effect, such as the boil and swirl of the unison strings in the coda of the *Leonora No. 3*, the source of which is Cherubini's *Elisa* overture; 'alarm' effects; brusque repetitive figures that seem to keep clashing with each other between two walls; sequences of syncopated chords (here the resemblance is striking) employed at the same moment and in the same place in the coda of the *Leonora No. 2* and in that of *Elisa*; unquestionable analogies of complementary rhythms in the *Leonora No. 1*, the *Fidelio No. 4*, the *Coriolan* on the one hand and Cherubini's *Elisa* and Méhul's *Stratonice* on the other; resemblances between certain themes in Méhul's overtures and in those of Beethoven; and so on. Lastly, the idea of the tremendous trumpet fanfare in the *Leonora No. 2* and *Leonora No. 3* came from Méhul's overture to *Hélène*!

But here we become more than ever conscious of the magic power of genius. It is nothing to have ideas: the thing is to realise them. And for the realisation of them neither intelligence, nor a fine sense of art, nor skill in form, necessary as all these are, is enough; these are only the portico. Enter the building and erect the vault! Each of the really remarkable suggestions

* Neues Beethoven — Jahrbuch, 1925: Cherubinis Einfluss auf Beethovens Ouvertüren

of Méhul or Cherubini is merely the invitation to proceed along a certain path; they draw back at the first step, but Beethoven presses on. Passion does not merely suggest; it demands the complete embrace! Cherubini recoils; he is too intelligent not to know what he is letting slip from his grasp, but he doubts his own strength; he turns away from the lovely form, and is satisfied to sketch a noble intellectual portrait of it. His themes lack blood, his melodies are abstract: he has formulated the rules of the game clearly enough, but he will not risk the hazard of it. Beethoven throws the whole of himself into it. And into this inferno of the soul — passions, combats, sufferings — that the musicians of the Revolution have indeed known but have not dared to enter, Beethoven, following in their track, boldly penetrates, and, leaving them on the threshold, descends to the depths.

☆

The descent into the abyss and the subsequent ascent out of the night into full sunlight: this is the dominant impression produced by *Leonora*. The tragic contrast and the *crescendo* of light are realised with perfect mastery, however, only in the second part of the first act — after Leonora's famous aria. Until then Beethoven has been hesitating, searching; as yet he has caught only a glimpse of his true subject and when suddenly it dawns upon him: '*Ach! brich noch nicht, du mattes Herz!*' he is overwhelmed, transported into a completely different world of music. It is too late now to re-establish the transition from Singspiel to opera, from the comedy of everyday life to high tragedy! Certainly that task was not an easy one: but it was not above the capacity of a Beethoven. Mozart had accomplished it, and even Gluck, whose *Iphigenia in Aulis* and *Orfeo* are a harmonious blend of the highest lyrical forms and the simplest, the most popular.

But *Leonora* was for Beethoven a first essay; when he began it he was entering a *terra ignota*. And his natural mistake was that, for lack of power to take in the whole of this new continent with one of those eagle glances that, in the *Eroica* or the C minor, survey the whole field of battle, he prudently set himself to begin at the beginning. He followed the order of the 'numbers' with exemplary patience and unexampled tenacity, constraining his herculean muscles to turn the spinning-wheel of the little Marcellina, to copy Mozart in the familiar domestic scenes, to array his giant music in the hoods of the puppets of the little song-plays of Leipzig or Paris.

It goes without saying that a labour of this kind cannot be absolutely in vain in the case of a Beethoven; and these introductory numbers are distinguished by some fine details of orchestration, some delicate expressions of feeling. Particularly successful are the quartet in canon, — the vocalised evolution of which was not lost on the young Berlioz of *Benvenuto Cellini* — and the duet between Marcellina and Leonora, with its innocent tenderness and its charming orchestral ornamentation.

But it is evident that Beethoven's heart is not in his work as yet, that he is writing like a pupil of the Singspiel elegants. The whole of this first part of the first act, this half-way house in which Mozart was thoroughly at home, is cold, and imitative not of nature but of books. Even in the second half of the act the scenes and characters that do not lie close to the thoughts and passions of Beethoven are only half-successful. Pizarro is a traitor of melodrama, not lacking in savage grandeur (Weber did not forget him),

33

but with a touch of the ridiculous about him. And in the first version of the end of the first act (Pizarro, Rocco, Leonora: Pizarro and his bodyguard) some fairly new and moving pages are combined with the heavy conventions of pompous declamatory opera, — a sort of Meyerbeer *avant la lettre*. It is the revenge, we might almost say the punishment, of sincerity. Beethoven cannot lie: an artistic nature like his is completely unable to simulate emotions it has not experienced. By the very nature of his being he must love, hate, believe, take fire. Nothing by halves: everything in extremes.

He might have made a frank plunge into the very centre of the drama with Leonora's aria and the Prisoners' scene; but to do that he would have needed the support of some great librettist formed in the school of Gluck. He had around him none but mediocrities, hangers-on of the theatre, who were nowhere so much at their ease as in the insipid conventions that had been manipulated a thousand times already. Being a newcomer in the theatre, he lacked the authority to assail them as Gluck would have done. Still less had he Gluck's robust health, his weight of manner, that would have made it possible for him to ascend the stage and give battle with fist and tongue to this crew of routineers and liars, the actors, the singers, the chorus, the instrumentalists, the librettist, the producer! He was a sick man; he heard only half of what was going on; he ran the risk of having it said, 'Why do you interfere? You are deaf.' And so he accepted what was given him; he began with the established conventions.

But what we have to consider is not the point of departure but the point of arrival. These conventions that he so meekly and unwillingly endorses, this formal frock-coat in which his great chest suffocates during the first ten numbers — see him burst them and tear them in pieces with a single stroke!

Thematic Guide

Many of the themes from the opera have been identified in the preceding articles by numbers in square brackets, which refer to the themes on these pages. The original numbers of the musical items in the full score have been noted in italics, and should not be confused with the numbers of the thematic guide. The numbers in square brackets also appear at relevant moments in the libretto so that the words can be related to the musical examples in the thematic guide.

[1] OVERTURE

[2]

[3] JACQUINO

Now, sweetheart as no-one is near, let's talk for a while here in priv-ate.

Jetzt, Schätzchen, jetzt sind wir all-ein, wir können vertraulich nun plau-dern.

[4] MARCELLINA

Oh were I now al-rea-dy wed that hus-band I might call you

O wär' ich schon mit dir—ver-eint und dür-fte Mann dich nen-nen!

[5] MARCELLINA

No words can tell the pure de-light, that hope al-rea-dy brings in sight,

Die Hoffnung füllt die Brust mit un-aus-sprechlich süs-ser Lust, schon er–

Andante sostenuto

sempre 𝆏

MARCELLINA

Andante sostenuto

sotto voce

Such strange de-light is here, my heart now weeps for me

Mir ist so wun - der - bar, es engt das Herz mir ein.

[8] ROCCO

Allegro moderato

If you lack for gold, my children then your home is full of care,

Hat man nicht auch Gold bei - ne - ben, kann man nicht ganz glücklich sein;

[9] ROCCO

Allegro

But when in your pockets you jin-gle your gold

Doch wenn's in den Taschen fein klin-gelt und rollt

[10] LEONORA

Allegro ma non troppo

True love's pre - pared to suf - fer tor - ture, suf———— fer

Kann Lie - be schon auch ho - he Lei - den, ho———— he

end————less tor———— ture.

Lei————den tra———— gen.

[11] LEONORA

Allegro ma non troppo

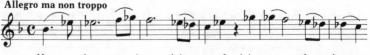

Now hope at — last brings com - fort brings com——fort here —

Du, Hoff - nung reichst mir La - bung, mir La——bung dar,

Allegro molto

L
Though bit-ter, bit-ter — tears — were — flowing.
Es kos-tet bitt'-re, bitt' — re— Tränen.

M
Tho' joy-ous tears— be— flow-(ing)
O süs-se, süs—— se — Trän-(en)

[13]
Allegro agitato

pp

|14| PIZARRO
Allegro agitato

Now, now, now, now the time has come my vengeance shall be sa - ted
Ha, ha, ha, welch ein Au-gen-blick! Die Rache werd ich küh - len!

[15] PIZARRO
Allegro con brio
mezza voce

Mur ——— der!
Mor ——— den!

[16] LEONORA
Adagio

Sweet hope, oh ne-ver let your star, your last faint star of com-fort be de-nied - me
Komm Hoff-nung, lass den letzten Stern, den letzten Stern der Müden er -blei – chen!
nicht

Oh what de- light
O wel-che Lust

[17]
Allegro ma non troppo

O what de-light
O wel-che Lust

Oh what de-light to breathe the air,
O wel — che Lust in frei er Luft, Luft

Oh what de- light — Oh what de light to breathe the air,
O wel -che Lust — in frei - er Luft, in frei - er Luft

37

Allegro ma non troppo

We trust for our de - liv'rance in Hea - ven's help - in Heaven's
helpand guidance

Wir woll - en mit ver - trau - en auf Gott - es Hi - lfe, auf Gottes Hilfe bauen!

[19] ROCCO
Andante con moto

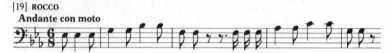

No time to waste, we must get ready.   I'll need your help, keep calm and steady.

Wir müssen gleich zu Werke schreiten,   du musst mir helf - en, mich be - glei-ten.

[20] MARCELLINA
Allegro molto

Oh fa ———————— ther, father dear.

Ach, Va ———————— ter, Vater, eilt!

[21] PIZARRO
Allegro molto

Pre - sump ———— tuous scoundrel
do you dare com - mit such an out - rage as I see?

Ver - weg ———— ner Alte welche Rech - te legst du dir frevelnd selber bei?

[22] PRISONERS
Allegretto vivace

Fare - well to spring and heaven's light,   joys   all too soon de - nied us

Leb wohl, du war - mes Son - nen - licht, schnell schwindest du uns wie - der

[23] FLORESTAN

Recit.

God!   what end—less   night!

Gott!   Welch Dun-kel   hier!

[24] **FLORESTAN**
Poco Allegro **Adagio**

I'll not com-plain. I must suf —————— fer, lies with Thee.
Ich mur-re nicht! Dass Mass der Lei —————— den steht bei dir.

[25] **FLORESTAN**
Adagio

In the spring of life's young morning all my joy de-par ———— ted
In des Leb - ens Frühlings tag - en ist das Glück von mir ————— geflohn!

[26] **FLORESTAN**
Poco Allegro

What gen-tle, soft breezes a-round me now play? What brightens my grave with such splendour?
Und spür ich nicht linde, sanft säuseln - de Luft? Und ist nicht mein Grab mir er hellet?

[27]
Andante con moto

[28] **FLORESTAN**
Moderato

Some bet - ter world, one day — re — ward you
Euch wer - de Lohn in be — ssern — Welten,

[29] **PIZARRO**
Allegro

Pi - zarro, whom you have ruined Pi - zarro
Pi - zarro, den du stür-zen wolltest, Pi - zarro

would

[30] **LEONORA**
Allegro

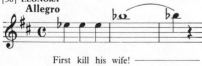

First kill his wife! —————
Töt erst sein weib! —————

Un poco sostenuto

[32]

Un poco sostenuto

[33] LEONORA

Allegro vivace

Oh   sweet de -   light   beyond   all   telling!

O   na - men,   na - menlo - se   Freude!

[34] FERNANDO

Un poco maestoso

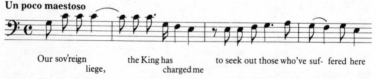

Our sov'reign   the King has   to seek out those who've suf- fered here
liege,   charged me

Des besten Kö——nigs Wink und   führt mich zu euch, ihr Ar—men, her,
Wil - le

[35]

Sostenuto assai

Alberto Remedios as Florestan at ENO (photo: Andrew March)

Josephine Barstow as Leonora at ENO (photo: Andrew March)

Fidelio

Opera in two acts

Music by Ludwig van Beethoven
Libretto after Jean-Nicolas Bouilly
by Josef Sonnleithner, Stefan von Breuning
and Georg Friedrich Treitschke
English version: Lyrics Tom Hammond
Dialogue Rodney Blumer

This text of *Fidelio* is the authentic libretto for the final (1814) version of the opera. It is written in an old-fashioned German style which sounds distinctly melodramatic to the modern reader. It includes much dialogue which is very rarely (if ever) now performed and original stage directions which do not necessarily describe the ENO or any other modern production. For the new ENO production in May 1980, the English version of the lyrics was especially revised and the entire dialogue was freshly translated (for performance in a shortened form). The translation of the complete dialogue of Fidelio was, however, undertaken especially for this Guide and it was never intended for performance. This almost literal translation provided the basis for the performing version used by ENO, which was also the product of many revisions in the course of rehearsal. Alterations were, inevitably, also made to the lyrics in that period as well, of which as many as possible have been incorporated.

The musical numbers which follow the stage directions after an oblique are those in the full score. The numbers in square brackets refer to the Thematic Guide.

Fidelio was first performed at the Theater an der Wien, Vienna on November 20, 1805. The first version was then revised and produced in a second edition on March 29, 1806. A third and final version was made for a revival on May 23, 1814. That version was first performed in England at the King's Theatre, Haymarket on May 18, 1832 and in the USA at the Park Theatre, New York on September 9, 1839. *Fidelio* was first given by Sadler's Wells Opera in 1937. *Leonora* (the first version) was given at the London Coliseum in 1970.

THE CHARACTERS

Don Fernando *Minister*	bass-baritone
Don Pizarro *Governor of a State prison*	baritone
Florestan *a prisoner*	tenor
Leonora (Leonore) *his wife, using the name of 'Fidelio'*	soprano
Rocco	bass
Marcellina (Marzelline) *his daughter*	soprano
Jacquino (Jaquino) *porter*	tenor
First Prisoner	tenor
Second Prisoner	bass

Captain of the Watch, Officers, Soldiers, State-prisoners, People

Fidelio

The action takes place in a State Prison, some miles from Seville, in the eighteenth century.

Act One

The courtyard of the State Prison. In the background the main gate and a high wall with ramparts over which trees are visible. In the gate itself, which is shut, there is a little wicket which is opened for occasional visitors on foot. Near the gate is the porter's lodge. The wings on the left represent the prisoners' cells; all the windows are barred and the doors, which are numbered, are reinforced with iron and shuttered with heavy bolts. In the forwardmost wing is the door to the gaoler's quarters. On the right there are trees protected by iron railings, and these, with a garden gate, show the entrance to the castle gardens.

Scene One. *Marcellina is ironing laundry in front of her door; at her side is a brazier on which she warms the iron. Jacquino stands close to his lodge; he opens the door to various people who hand him parcels, which he puts in his lodge. | Duet No. 1 [2]*

JACQUINO
(ardently rubbing his hands)

Now, sweetheart, as no-one is near,	[3] Jetzt, Schätzchen, jetzt sind wir allein,
Let's talk for a while here in private.	Wir können vertraulich nun plaudern.

MARCELLINA
(continuing her work)

No time to be serious, I fear,	Es wird wohl nichts Wichtiges sein,
I daren't stop my work for a moment.	Ich darf bei der Arbeit nicht zaudern.

JACQUINO

Well listen, you obstinate girl!	Ein Wörtchen, du Trotzige, du!

MARCELLINA

Speak up then, I'm list'ning you'll find.	So sprich nur, ich höre ja zu.

JACQUINO

If you'll not be friendlier towards me	Wenn du mir nicht freundlicher blickest,
Then I cannot think what to say.	So bring ich kein Wörtchen hervor.

MARCELLINA

If you dislike my demeanour	Wenn du dich nicht in mich schickest,
I'll stop up my ears right away!	Verstopf ich mir vollends das Ohr.
You'll give me no peace, I can see,	So hab' ich denn nimmermehr Ruh;
Let's hear what you're longing to say!	So rede, so rede nur zu.

JACQUINO

Oh spare me a moment, I pray,	Ein Weilchen nur höre mir zu,
And then I will go right away.	Dann lass ich dich wieder in Ruh.
I've . . . I've chosen . . .	Ich, ich habe,
I've chosen to make you my wedded wife,	Ich habe zum Weib dich gewählet,
You follow?	Verstehst du?

MARCELLINA

That's all very clear.	Das ist ja doch klar.

JACQUINO

If you say you're willing to take me	Und, und wenn mir dein Jawort nicht fehlet,

Then we'd make . . .   Was meinst du?

MARCELLINA

A fine loving pair.   So sind wir ein Paar.

JACQUINO

A month then and we could be   Wir könnten in wenigen Wochen . . .
married . . .

MARCELLINA

Bravo, so you've settled the day!   Recht schön, du bestimmst schon die Zeit!
(knocking is heard)

JACQUINO
(to himself)

Oh curse them they never stop knocking,   Zum Henker das ewige Pochen!
And just when success seemed so near,   Da war ich so herrlich im Gang,
That always evades me I fear.   Und immer entwischt mir der Fang.

MARCELLINA
(to herself)

At last he will leave me in peace!   So bin ich doch endlich befreit!
I'm bored by his passion, I fear   Wie macht seine Liebe mir bang,
How tedious his signs now appear!   Und wie werden die Stunden mir lang.

Jacquino opens the wicket, takes a parcel and places it in his lodge; meanwhile Marcellina works on.

MARCELLINA

I know all the lad must be suff'ring   Ich weiss, dass der Arme sich quälet,
I pity, yes pity his sighs, alas!   Es tut mir so leid auch um ihn!
Fidelio now I have chosen   Fidelio hab' ich gewählet,
His love is the treasure I prize.   Ihn lieben ist süsser Gewinn.

JACQUINO
(coming back)

Where was I? She won't look my way.   Wo war ich? Sie sieht mich nicht an!

MARCELLINA
(aside)

He's back, then – he'll start up again!   Da is er – er fängt wieder an!

JACQUINO
(aside)

Now when will you give me your answer?   Wann wirst du das Jawort mir geben?
It could be this morning you know.   Es könnte ja heute noch sein.

MARCELLINA
(aside)

Oh God, I shall soon lose my temper!   O weh! er verbittert mein Leben!
(aloud)

This morning, tomorrow and always my   Jetzt, morgen und immer nein, nein!
answer is no, no.

JACQUINO

You must have a heart made of stone,   Du bist doch wahrhaftig von Stein,
No love or compassion you show.   Kein Wünschen, kein Bitten geht ein.

MARCELLINA
(aside)

I'm forced to be hard, that I know,   Ich muss ja so hart mit ihn sein,
He builds on the slightest of hopes.   Er hofft bei dem mindesten Schein.

So you're firm in this sudden decision?	So wirst du dich nimmer bekehren?
Come, tell me!	Was meinst du?

When will you be gone?	Du könntest nun gehn.

What?	Wie?
Just watching you, is that forbidden,	Dich anzusehen willst du mir wehren?
What that too?	Auch das noch?

Oh stay and have done.	So bleibe hier stehn.

You know that you frequently promised . . .	Du hast mir so oft doch versprochen . . .

I promised? Now you go too far!	Versprochen? Nein, das geht zu weit!

(knocking is heard)

(to himself)

Damnation! They never stop knocking!	Zum Henker das ewige Pochen!

(to herself)

At last I'll be left here in peace	So bin ich doch endlich befreit!
That sound is most welcome to hear.	Das ist ein wilkommener Klang,
I really was frightened to death, then, I fear.	Es wurde zu Tode mir bang.

I've really surprised her that's clear,	Es ward ihr im Ernste schon bang,
Who knows, success might have been near.	Wer weiss, ob es mir nicht gelang.

Another parcel is delivered.

If I haven't opened that door two hundred times already today then my name's not Caspar Eustace Jacquino.	Wenn ich diese Tür heute nicht schon zweihundertmal aufgemacht habe, so will ich nicht Kaspar Eustach Jaquino heissen.

(to Marcellina)

Now at last I can talk again.	Endlich kann ich doch wieder einmal plaudern.

(knocking is heard)

Damnation! Not again!	Zum Wetter! schon wieder!

He goes to open the door.

(downstage)

How can I help it if I don't like him as much as I used to?	Was kann ich dafür, dass ich ihn nicht mehr so gern wie sonst haben kann?

(to the person who knocked, as he quickly shuts the door)

I'll take care of it, right away.	Ich werde es besorgen. Schon recht!

(going up to Marcellina)

Now I won't let anyone disturb us.	So! – Nun, hoffe ich, soll niemand mehr uns stören.

ROCCO
(calling from the garden)

Jacquino! Jacquino!	Jaquino! Jaquino!

MARCELLINA

Don't you hear? Father's calling.	Hörst du? Der Vater ruft!

JACQUINO

Let him wait a little. I mean . . . about our love . . .	Lassen wir ihn ein wenig warten. Also, auf unsere Liebe zu kommen –

MARCELLINA

Go to him. Father will be wanting news of Fidelio.	So geh doch. Der Vater wird sich nach Fidelio erkundigen wollen.

JACQUINO
(jealously)

Oh well, of course then, no one can move fast enough . . .	Ei freilich, da kann man nicht schnell genug sein.

ROCCO
(calling again)

Jacquino! Don't you hear?	Jaquino, hörst du nicht?

JACQUINO
(calling)

I'm coming.	Ich komme schon!

(to Marcellina)

Just wait here, I'll be back with you in two minutes.	Bleib fein hier, in zwei Minuten sind wir weider beisammen.

Exit to the garden through the open door. **Scene Two.** *Marcellina alone.*

MARCELLINA

Poor Jacquino – I'm almost sorry for him. But can I do anything about it? I *was* quite fond of him, but then Fidelio came to live with us and since then everything's changed.	Der arme Jaquino dauert mich beinahe. Kann ich es aber ändern? Ich war ihm sonst recht gut, da kam Fidelio in unser Haus, und seit der Zeit ist alles in mir und um mich verändert. Ach!

She heaves a heavy sigh.

And just through feeling sorry for Jacquino I see now how fond I am of Fidelio. I think he's fond of me too, and if only I knew what my father thought, then perhaps my happiness would be complete.	Aus dem Mitleiden, das ich mit Jaquino habe, merke ich erst, wie sehr gut ich Fidelio bin. Ich glaube auch, dass Fidelio mir recht gut ist, und wenn ich die Gesinnungen des Vaters wüsste, so könnte vielleicht mein Glück bald vollkommen werden.

Aria No. 2

MARCELLINA [4]

Oh, were I now already wed, That husband I might call you. A girl may only half confess The secret of her feelings. Then I would never blush to own The kiss that makes you mine alone	O wär ich schon mit dir vereint Und dürfte Mann dich nennen! Ein Mädchen darf ja, was es meint, Zur Hälfte nur bekennen. Doch wenn ich nicht erröten muss, Ob einem warmen Herzenskuss

48

And tears were left behind me! No words can tell the pure delight That hope already brings in sight, How happy love would find me.	Wenn nichts uns stört auf Erden — [5] Die Hoffnung schon erfüllt die Brust, Mit unaussprechlich süsser Lust, Wie glücklich will ich werden!
Throughout our simple daily life, With joy I'd face each morrow. For then the smiles of man and wife Would banish ev'ry sorrow. When all the work of day is done, And night has veiled the setting sun And he was close beside me, No words can tell the pure delight That hope already brings in sight How happy love would find me.	In Ruhe stiller Häuslichkeit Erwach ich jeden Morgen, Wir grüssen uns mit Zärtlichkeit, Der Fleiss verscheucht die Sorgen. Und ist die Arbeit abgetan, Dann schleicht die holde Nacht heran, Dann ruhn wir von Beschwerden. Die Hoffnung schon erfüllt die Brust Mit unaussprechlich süsser Lust, Wie glücklich will ich werden!

Scene Three. *Marcellina, Rocco, Jacquino. Rocco comes out of the garden. Behind him Jacquino carries gardening tools, which he takes into Rocco's house.*

ROCCO

Good morning Marcellina. Is Fidelio not back yet?	Guten Tag, Marzelline. Ist Fidelio noch nicht zurückgekommen?

MARCELLINA

No, father.	Nein, Vater.

ROCCO

The time's coming for me to take to the governor the despatches that Fidelio's supposed to be bringing. I await him with impatience.	Die Stunde naht, wo ich dem Gouverneur die Briefschaften bringen muss, welche Fidelio abholen sollte. Ich erwarte ihn mit Ungeduld.

During these last words there was a knocking at the door.

JACQUINO
(coming out of Rocco's house)

I'm coming.	Ich komme schon!

(he runs officiously to open it)

MARCELLINA

He'll have had to wait such a long time at the blacksmith's.	Er wird gewiss so lange bei dem Schmied haben warten müssen.

Meanwhile she has seen Leonora come through the door. Gaily.

There he is!	Da ist er!

Scene Four. *The same, Leonora. Enter Leonora. She wears a dark jerkin, a red waistcoat, dark breeches, short boots, a broad belt of black leather with a copper buckle: her hair is worn in a net cap. On her back, she carries a box of provisions and in her arms are chains which she leaves at the porter's lodge as she enters; at her side hangs a metal tin on a cord.*

MARCELLINA
(running up to Leonora)

How he's loaded down! Dear God! The sweat's running down his brow.	Wie er belastet ist. Lieber Gott! Der Schweiss läuft ihm von der Stirn.

She takes her handkerchief and tries to wipe Leonora's brow.

ROCCO

Wait, wait.	Warte! Warte!

He helps Marcellina to take the box off Leonora's back and place it in the lefthand arcade.

JACQUINO
(aside, downstage)

Well, that was worth the bother of opening up so quickly to let the 'young master' in.	Es war auch der Mühe wert, so schnell aufzumachen, um den Patron da hereinzulassen.

He goes into his lodge but soon comes out as though about his business, yet really trying to keep an eye on Marcellina, Leonora and Rocco.

ROCCO
(to Leonora)

Poor Fidelio, this time you've loaded yourself up too much.	Armer Fidelio, diesmal hast du dir zuviel aufgeladen.

LEONORA
(coming forward and wiping her face)

I must confess I am a little tired. The smith took so long mending the fetters that I thought he'd never be done.	Ich muss gestehen, ich bin ein wenig ermüdet. Der Schmied hatte an den Ketten so lange auszubessern, dass ich glaubte, er würde nicht damit fertig werden.

ROCCO

Has he done them properly?	Sind sie jetzt gut gemacht?

LEONORA

Oh yes, they're good and strong. None of the prisoners will be able to break them now.	O gewiss, recht gut and stark. Keiner der Gefangenen wird sie zerbrechen.

ROCCO

And how much did all th ; cost?	Wieviel kostet alles zusammen?

LEONORA

About twelve piastres. Here is the detailed account.	Zwölf Piaster ungefähr. Hier ist die genaue Berechnung.

ROCCO
(checking the bill)

Good. Well done. Good heavens, there are things here we'll be able to get twice as much back on. You're a clever boy. I can't even understand how you do your reckoning. You buy everything more cheaply than I. In the six months since I've put you in charge of the stores you've made more than ever I did in a whole year.	Gut, brav! Zum Wetter! Da gibt's Artikel, auf denen wir wenigstens das Doppelte gewinnen können. Du bist ein kluger Junge! Ich kann gar nicht begreifen, wie du deine Rechnungen machst. Du kaufst alles wohlfeiler als ich. In den sechs Monaten, seit ich dir die Anschaffung der Lebensmittel übertrug, hast du mehr gewonnen als ich vorher in einem ganzen Jahr.

(aside)

The rascal's obviously going to all this trouble on account of my Marcellina.	Der Schelm gibt sich alle diese Mühe offenbar meiner Marzelline wegen.

LEONORA

I try to do what I can.	Ich suche zu tun, was mir möglich ist.

ROCCO

Yes, yes, you're a good lad, you couldn't be more zealous or prudent. I grow to like you more every day that passes and	Ja, ja, du bist brav, man kann nicht eifriger, nicht verständiger sein. Ich habe dich aber auch mit jedem Tage

| – rest assured, your reward will not be slow. | lieber und — sei versichert, dein Lohn soll nicht ausbleiben. |

During the last words, he glances from Leonora to Marcellina.

LEONORA
(disconcerted)

| Don't think I do my duty just for reward . . . | O glaubt nicht, dass ich meine Schuldigkeit nur des Lohnes wegen — |

ROCCO

| Hush now! | Still! |

(looking at them as before)

| D'you think I can't see into your heart? | Meinst du, ich könnte dir nicht ins Herz sehen? |

He appears to take pleasure in Leonora's increasing embarrassment and then goes to one side to examine the chains. / Quartet No. 3 [6]

MARCELLINA
(while Rocco considers Leonora approvingly, Marcellina watches and sings to herself)

Such strange delight is here,	[7] Mir ist so wunderbar,
My heart now weeps for me.	Es engt das Herz mir ein.
He loves me that is clear,	Er liebt mich, es ist klar,
How happy I shall be.	Ich werde glücklich sein.

LEONORA
(aside)

How great the danger here.	Wie gross ist die Gefahr,
Faint hope is left for me.	Wie schwach der Hoffnung Schein.
She loves me, that is clear,	Sie liebt mich, es ist klar,
How harsh and cruel fate can be.	O namenlose Pein!

ROCCO
(during the foregoing, Rocco comes downstage and sings to himself)

She loves him, that is clear,	Sie liebt ihn, es ist klar,
Her husband he shall be.	Ja Mädchen, er wird dein.
They'll make a handsome pair,	Ein gutes, junges Paar,
How happy they will be.	Sie werden glücklich sein.

JACQUINO
(watching them and moving closer and closer to the side, a little behind the others)

My heart is numb with fear,	Mir sträubt sich schon das Haar,
Her father's choice I see,	Der Vater willigt ein,
To me she's ever dear,	Mir wird so wunderbar;
What chance remains for me?	Mir fällt kein Mittel ein.

Jacquino returns to his lodge.

ROCCO

| Listen Fidelio, even though I don't know where you come from or who your father was, I know what I'll do, I'm going to take you as my son-in-law. | Höre, Fidelio, wenn ich auch nicht weiss, wie und wo du auf die Welt gekommen bist, und wenn du auch gar keinen Vater gehabt hättest, so weiss ich doch, was ich tue - ich - ich mache dich zu meinem Tochtermann. |

MARCELLINA
(quickly)

| And will you do it soon, dear father? | Wirst du es bald tun, lieber Vater? |

(laughing)

Ay ay, how eager!	Ei, ei, wie eilfertig!

(more seriously)

When the governor's gone to Seville we'll have more time. You know he has to go every month to give account of everything that happens in the prison. In a few days he'll be off again, and the day after his departure I'll see you married. You can count on that.

Sobald der Gouverneur nach Sevilla gereist sein wird, dann haben wir mehr Musse. Ihr wisst ja, dass er alle Monate hingeht, um über alles, was hier in dem Staatsgefängnis vorfällt, Rechenschaft zu geben. In einigen Tagen muss er wieder fort, und den Tag nach seiner Abreise gebe ich euch zusammen. Darauf könnt ihr rechnen.

MARCELLINA

The day after his departure? That's very sensible, dear father.

Den Tag nach seiner Abreise? Das machst du vernünftig, lieber Vater.

LEONORA
(disconcerted, then cheerfully)

The day after his departure?

Den Tag nach seiner Abreise?

(aside)

Yet another complication!

O welche neue Verlegenheit!

ROCCO

So, my children, you really are in love with each other, aren't you? But that's not everything that's needed for a really solid and happy household; you also need . . .

Nun, meine Kinder, ihr habt euch doch recht herzlich lieb, nicht wahr? Aber das ist noch nicht alles, was zu einer guten, vergnügten Haushaltung gehört; man braucht auch –

He makes the gesture of counting money.| Aria No. 4

ROCCO

If you lack for gold, my children,
Then your home is full of care,
You will find that life is cheerless,
Gloomy days you both must share.
But when in your pockets you jingle your gold,
You'll find what a fortune you're making,
Then love and power and pleasure untold,

Will always be yours for the taking!
Good luck's a slave that's bought and sold,
Oh what a glorious thing is gold.

[8] Hat man nicht auch Gold beineben,
Kann man nicht ganz glücklich sein;
Traurig schleppt sich fort das Leben,
Mancher Kummer stellt sich ein.
Doch wenn's in den Taschen fein
[9] klingelt und rollt,
Da hält man das Schicksal gefangen,
Und Macht und Liebe verschafft dir das Gold
Und stillet das kühnste Verlangen.
Das Glück dient wie ein Knecht für Sold,
Es ist ein schönes Ding, das Gold.

If your purse is always empty,
Then you'll never pay your way.
What's the use of love in plenty,
When you're hungry ev'ry day?
May smiling good fortune its favours unfold,
And prosper your ev'ry endeavour,
Your sweetheart beside you, your purse full of gold,
Then you could be happy for ever.
Good luck's a slave that's bought and sold,

Wenn sich Nichts mit Nichts verbindet,
Ist und bleibt die Summe klein;
Wer bei Tisch nur Liebe findet,
Wird nach Tische hungrig sein.
Drum lächle der Zufall euch gnädig und hold,
Und segne und lenk' euer Streben;
Das Liebchen im Arme, im Beutel das Gold,
So mögt ihr viel Jahre durchleben.
Das Glück dient wie ein Knecht für Sold,

Oh what a glorious thing is gold.	Es ist ein mächtig Ding, das Gold.

LEONORA

That's easily said, master Rocco, but I, I believe that the union of two hearts that feel alike is the source of true happiness.	Ihr könnt das leicht sagen, Meister Rocco, aber ich, ich behaupte, dass die Vereinigung zweier gleichgestimmter Herzen die Quelle des wahren ehelichen Glückes ist.

(warmly)

That happiness must be the greatest joy on earth!	O dieses Glück muss der grösste Schatz auf Erden sein!

(catching herself, and restraining herself)

Though I must admit there is something that would be hardly less precious to me, though I'm sad that in spite of all my efforts I am not going to win it.	Freilich gibt es noch etwas, was mir nicht weniger kostbar sein würde, aber mit Kummer sehe ich, dass ich es durch alle meine Bemühungen nicht erhalten werde.

ROCCO

And what might that be?	Und was wäre denn das?

LEONORA

Your trust! Forgive me this little reproach, but how often have I seen you coming up from the underground vaults of this fortress out of breath and exhausted. Why won't you let me go with you? I would like so much to help you with your work and be able to share your burden.	Euer Vertrauen! Verzeiht mir diesen kleinen Vorwurf, aber oft sehe ich Euch aus den unterirdischen Gewölben dieses Schlosses ganz ausser Atem und ermattet zurück kommen. Warum erlaubt Ihr mir nicht, Euch dahin zu begleiten? Es wäre mir so lieb, wenn ich Euch bei Eurer Arbeit helfen und Eure Beschwerden teilen könnte.

ROCCO

You know quite well I'm under strictest orders to let no one, whoever they may be, near the prisoners of state.	Du weisst doch, dass ich den strengsten Befehl habe, niemanden, wer es auch sein mag, zu den Staatsgefangenen zu lassen.

MARCELLINA

But there are far too many of them in this fortress. You're working yourself to death, father dear.	Es sind ihrer aber gar zu viele in dieser Festung. Du arbeitest dich ja zu Tode, lieber Vater.

LEONORA

She is right, master Rocco. Duty must be done;	Sie hat recht, Meister Rocco. Man soll allerdings seine Schuldigkeit tun;

(affectionately)

but sometimes we are allowed to think, surely, of sparing ourselves a little for those who love us and depend on us.	aber es ist doch auch erlaubt, mein ich, zuweilen daran zu denken, wie man sich für die, die uns angehören und lieben, ein bisschen schonen kann.

She presses his hand into hers.

MARCELLINA

(pressing Rocco's other hand to her breast)

Everyone has a duty to keep well for the sake of their children.	Man muss sich für seine Kinder zu erhalten suchen.

ROCCO
(looking at them both with emotion)

You're right, in the end this heavy task will be too much for me. However strict the Governor may be, he must let me take you with me to the secret dungeons.

Ja, ihr habt recht, diese schwere Arbeit würde mir doch endlich zuviel werden. Der Gouverneur ist zwar sehr streng, er muss mir aber doch erlauben, dich in die geheimen Kerker mit mir zu nehmen.

Leonora makes a violent gesture of joy.

And yet, there's *one* vault I'll never be allowed to show you, even though I can rely on you completely.

Indessen gibt es ein Gewölbe, in das ich dich wohl nie werde führen dürfen, obschon ich mich ganz auf dich verlassen kann.

MARCELLINA

That must be the one with the prisoner you've told us about so often?

Vermutlich, wo der Gefangene sitzt, von dem du schon einige Male gesprochen hast?

ROCCO

You have guessed.

Du hast's erraten.

LEONORA
(enquiring)

I suppose he's been imprisoned for a long time?

Ich glaube, es ist schon lange her, dass er gefangen ist?

ROCCO

More than two years.

Es ist schon über zwei Jahre.

LEONORA
(vehemently)

Two years, d'you say?

Zwei Jahre, sagt Ihr?

(catching herself)

He must be a dangerous criminal.

Er muss ein grosser Verbrecher sein.

ROCCO

Or he must have dangerous enemies. It comes to much the same thing.

Oder er muss grosse Feinde haben, das kommt ungefähr auf eins heraus.

MARCELLINA

Hasn't anyone been able to find out where he comes from or who he is?

So hat man denn nie erfahren können, woher er ist und wie er heisst?

ROCCO

He's often tried to talk about it.

O wie oft hat er mit mir von alledem reden wollen.

LEONORA

And?

Nun?

ROCCO

For people like us it's best to know as few secrets as possible. So I've never listened to him. I might have blabbered it out, and that wouldn't have helped him anyway.

Für unsereinen ist's aber am besten, so wenig Geheimnisse als möglich zu wissen, darum hab ich ihn auch nie angehört. Ich hätte mich verplappern können, und ihm hätte ich doch, nicht genützt.

(confidentially)

But he won't be a burden to me much longer. It can't last long now.

Nun, er wird mich nicht lange mehr quälen. Es kann nicht mehr lange mit ihm dauern.

LEONORA
(aside)

Oh God!   Grosser Gott!

MARCELLINA

Dear heaven, how can he have deserved   Lieber Himmel! Wie hat er denn eine so
so heavy a punishment?   schwere Strafe verdient?

ROCCO
(even more confidentially)

For a month now on Don Pizarro's   Seit einem Monat schon muss ich auf
orders I've been steadily reducing his   Pizarros Befehl seine Portion immer
rations. Now he has no more than two   kleiner machen. Jetzt hat er binnen
ounces of bread and a half measure of   vierundzwanzig Stunden nicht mehr als
water every twenty-four hours. No light   zwei Unzen schwarzes Brot und ein halb
save for a lamp, no straw, nothing . . . Mass Wasser; kein Licht als den Schein
                                          einer Lampe – kein Stroh mehr – nichts –

MARCELLINA

Father, don't take Fidelio down there, he   O lieber Vater, führe Fidelio ja nicht zu
couldn't bear the sight!   ihm! Diesen Anblick könnte er nicht
                                             ertragen.

LEONORA

Why not? I have both the strength and   Warum denn nicht? Ich habe Mut and
the courage!   Stärke!

ROCCO
(patting her on the shoulder)

Well spoken my boy, well spoken. I   Brav, mein Sohn, brav! Wenn ich dir
could tell you how I had to wrestle with erzählen wollte, wie ich anfangs in
my conscience when I started this job.   meinem Stande mit meinem Herzen zu
And I was quite a different sort of fellow kämpfen hatte! – Und ich war doch ein
from you, with your smooth skin and   ganz anderer Kerl als du mit deiner
your soft hands.   feinen Haut und deinen weichen Händen .

Trio No. 5

ROCCO

Well said, young man,   Gut, Söhnchen, gut,
But keep your head,   Hab' immer Mut,
In all that lies before you,   Dann wird dir's auch gelingen;
And steel your heart   Das Herz wird hart
When you are faced with sights   Durch Gegenwart
That may appall you.   Bei fürchterlichen Dingen.

LEONORA
(vigorously)

I'm brave and strong,   Ich habe Mut!
Without a qualm.   Mit kaltem Blut
I'll venture down below there,   Will ich hinab mich wagen;
For rich reward,   Für hohen Lohn
True love's prepared   [10] Kann Liebe schon
To suffer any torture.   Auch hohe Leiden tragen.

MARCELLINA
(affectionately)

Your kindly heart   Dein gutes Herz
May feel distressed   Wird manchen Schmerz
By what you there discover;   In diesen Grüften leiden;
But here above,   Dann kehrt zurück

Return to love	Der liebe Glück
And all your joy recover!	Und unnennbare Freuden.

ROCCO

Your dearest hopes will soon be granted.	Du wirst dein Glück ganz sicher bauen.

LEONORA

My trust in God and right is planted.	Ich hab auf Gott und Recht Vertrauen.

MARCELLINA

I know your heart will not be daunted,	Du darfst mir auch in's Auge schauen;
The pow'r of Love is strong and sure.	Der Liebe Macht ist auch nicht klein.
Yes, a love that's strong and sure	Ja, wir werden glücklich sein.
Brings us joy for evermore.	

LEONORA

Yes, and yet may bring me joy.	Ja, ich kann noch glücklich sein.

ROCCO

Yes, a love that's strong and sure,	Ja, ihr werdet glücklich sein.
Brings us joy for evermore.	
My lord himself today must tell me	Der Gouverneur soll heut' erlauben,
That you may share my work with me.	Dass du mit mir die Arbeit teilst.

LEONORA

Of peace of mind you will deprive me	Du wirst mir alle Ruhe rauben,
If one more day's delay there be!	Wenn du bis morgen nur verweilst.

MARCELLINA

Yes, father ask this very morning	Ja, guter Vater, bitt' ihn heute,
Then we can wed without delay!	In kurzem sind wir dann ein Paar.

ROCCO

I fear my strength at last is failing,	Ich bin ja bald des Grabes Beute,
I need some help, yes, that is clear.	Ich brauche Hilf', es ist ja wahr.

LEONORA
(aside)

For long I've borne this bitter torment. . .	Wie lang bin ich des Kummers Beute!
Now Hope at last brings comfort here.	[11]Du, Hoffnung, reichst mir Labung dar.

MARCELLINA
(affectionately to Rocco)

Beloved father, what's this you say?	Ach, lieber Vater, was fällt euch ein?
You'll stay beside us for many a day.	Lang Freund und Rater müsst ihr uns sein.

ROCCO

If we take care, all will go well,	Nur auf der Hut, dann geht es gut,
And fears to joy will soon be turning.	Gestillt wird euer Sehnen.

MARCELLINA

Have no fear, when love is here,	O habe Mut, o welche Glut!
What deep, mysterious yearning!	O welch' ein tiefes Sehnen!

LEONORA

Kind words I hear, they calm my fear	Ihr seid so gut, ihr macht mir Mut,
And all my fevered yearning.	Gestillt wird bald mein Sehnen!

Come join your hands at love's	Gebt euch die Hand, und schliesst das Band
Command, tho' joyous tears be flowing.	In süssen Freudentränen.

LEONORA
(aside)

I gave my hand at love's command	Ich gab die Hand zum süssen Band,
Tho' bitter tears were flowing.	[12] Es kostet bitt're Tränen.

MARCELLINA

A lasting bond with heart and hand	Ein festes Band mit Herz und Hand!
Tho' joyous tears be flowing!	O süsse, süsse Tränen!

ROCCO

Now it's time for me to take the despatches to the Governor.	Aber nun ist es Zeit, dass ich dem Gouverneur die Briefschaften überbringe.

March No. 6
ROCCO

Ha! He's coming here himself!	Ah! Er kommt selbst hierher!

(to Leonora)

Give them to me Fidelio, and go.	Gib sie, Fidelio, und dann entfernt euch!

Leonora takes the tin box, gives it to Rocco, and goes into the house with Marcellina. During the march the main gate is opened from the outside by a sentry. Enter officers with a detachment, then Pizarro. The gate is shut behind him. **Scene Five.** *Pizarro. Officers. Watch.*

PIZARRO
(to the officers)

Three sentries to the ramparts, six guards day and night on the drawbridge, and as many by the postern. Anyone seen approaching the moat to be brought straight to me.	Drei Schildwachen auf den Wall! Sechs Mann Tag und Nacht an die Zugbrücke, ebenso viele gegen den Garten zu, und jedermann, der sich dem Graben der Festung nähert, werde sogleich vor mich gebracht!

(to Rocco)

Any news?	Ist etwas Neues vorgefallen?

ROCCO

No sir.	Nein, Herr.

PIZARRO

Despatches?	Wo sind die Depeschen?

ROCCO
(takes the letters from the tin box)

Here they are.	Hier sind sie.

PIZARRO
(opens the papers and goes through them)

Character references, complaints. If I took any notice of all this I'd never be finished.	Immer Empfehlungen oder Vorwürfe. Wenn ich auf alles das achten wollte, würde ich nie damit zu Ende kommen.

(stopping at one letter)

What's this? I seem to know this hand	Was seh'ich? Mich dünkt, ich kenne diese Schrift.

(opening the letter, and coming forward. Rocco and the Watch step back. He reads.)

'I herewith inform you that it has been	'Ich gebe Ihnen Nachricht, dass der

brought to the Minister's notice that in the State Prisons in your charge there are several victims of arbitrary exercise of power. He is setting out tomorrow for a surprise inspection. Be on your guard and see yourself safe.'

Minister in Erfahrung gebracht hat, dass die Staatsgefängnisse, denen Sie vorstehen, mehrere Opfer willkürlicher Gewalt enthalten. Er reist morgen ab, um Sie mit einer Untersuchung zu überraschen. Seien Sie auf Ihrer Hut und suchen Sie sich sicherzustellen.'

(disconcerted)

If he should discover that I have this Florestan lying in chains, him he thinks long since dead, this Florestan who sought to expose me to him, rob me of his favour . . . There is one remedy.

Ah, wenn er entdeckte, dass ich diesen Florestan in Ketten liegen habe, den er längst tot glaubt, ihn, der so oft meine Rache reizte, der mich vor dem Minister enthüllen und mir seine Gunst entziehen wollte. – Doch, es gibt ein Mittel!

(briskly)

Decisive action can dispel all anxiety.

Eine kühne Tat kann alle Besorgnisse zerstreuen!

Aria with Chorus No. 7 [13]

PIZARRO

Now, now the time has come,	[14] Ha! Welch' ein Augenblick!
My vengeance shall be sated.	Die Rache werd' ich kühlen,
Yes, fate demands his life,	Dich rufet dein Geschick!
I'll watch him die before me.	In seinem Herzen wühlen,
I'll stand no more delay,	O Wonne, grosses Glück!
Oh glorious, glorious day!	
Remember how once he made me	Schon war ich nah' im Staube,
The sport of men who hate me,	Dem lauten Spott zum Raube,
And then he brought me to disgrace,	Dahin gestreckt zu sein.
Yet, here in chains he's languished,	Nun ist es mir geworden,
The victor I have vanquished.	Den Mörder selbst zu morden.
And in his dying torment	In seiner letzten Stunde,
While he still writhes before me,	Den Stahl in seiner Wunde,
I'll shout into his ear	Ihm noch ins Ohr zu schrei'n:
That I now triumph here.	Triumph! Der Sieg ist mein!

SENTRIES' CHORUS
(under their breath)

His mood portends some danger,	Er spricht von Tod und Wunde!
Our rounds we'd best continue,	Nun fort auf uns're Runde!
Be careful, here's some affair of state.	Wie wichtig muss es sein!
His mood portends some danger,	Er spricht von Tod und Wunde!
Our rounds we'd best continue.	Wacht scharf auf eurer Runde!
Here's some affair of state.	Wie wichtig muss es sein!
Be careful, watch out.	

PIZARRO

Not a moment can I delay in making preparations for my plan. The Minister is expected today. Only the greatest care and speed can save me.

Ich darf keinen Augenblick säumen, alle Anstalten zu meinem Vorhaben zu treffen. Heute soll der Minister ankommen. Nur die grösste Vorsicht und Eile können mich retten.

(to the officer)

Captain! Listen.

Hauptmann! Hören Sie.

(leading him forward and speaking softly to him)

You are to climb the tower with the trumpeter at once. Watch the road from Seville with the utmost vigilance. As soon as you see a coach with outriders

Besteigen Sie mit einem Trompeter sogleich den Turm. Sehen Sie unablässig und mit der grössten Achtsamkeit auf die Strasse von Sevilla. Sobald Sie einen

approaching, have the signal sounded immediately. D'you understand? Immediately. I expect complete obedience. You will answer for it with your head.	Wagen von Reitern begleitet erblicken, lassen Sie augenblicklich ein Zeichen geben. Verstehn Sie, augenblicklich! Ich erwarte die grösste Pünktlichkeit. Sie haften mir mit Ihrem Kopf dafür.

(The officer leaves. Pizarro addresses the soldiers on watch.)

Away to your posts.	Fort auf eure Posten!

(The soldiers leave. Pizarro to Rocco.)

Old man!	Alter!

ROCCO

Sir.	Herr!

PIZARRO

(to himself, as he examines Rocco closely)

I must try to win him to me. Without his help I cannot see it through.	Ich muss ihn zu gewinnen suchen. Ohne seine Hilfe kann ich es nicht ausführen.

(aloud)

Come here.	Komm näher!

Duet No. 8

PIZARRO

Now Rocco! This matter's urgent, And fortune smiles upon you, You'll be a wealthy man.	Jetzt, Alter, hat es Eile! Dir wird ein Glück zu teile, Du wirst ein reicher Mann;

(throwing him a purse)

I'll give you that for now.	Das geb' ich nur daran.

ROCCO

But, tell me, if you please sir, What service must be done?	So sagt doch nur in Eile, Womit ich dienen kann.

PIZARRO

A man like you is wanted Your heart is still undaunted, Time's harden'd you still further.	Du bist von kalten Blute, Von unverzagtem Mute Durch langen Dienst geworden.

ROCCO

My task sir, tell me.	Was soll ich? Redet!

PIZARRO

Murder!	[15]	Morden!

ROCCO

Sir?	Wie?

PIZARRO

Listen to my plan. What's this? Are you a man? This cannot wait till later, The State itself may fall, A plot we must forestall, And kill a worthless traitor.	Höre mich nur an! Du bebst? Bist du ein Mann? Wir durfen gar nicht säumen; Dem Staate liegt daran, Den bösen Untertan Schnell aus dem Weg zu räumen.

ROCCO

My lord!	O Herr!

PIZARRO

You understand?	Du stehst noch an?

(aside)

While Florestan is living	Er darf nicht länger leben,
My danger's all too plain	Sonst ist's um mich geschehn.
Pizarro dare you falter?	Pizarro sollte beben?
He dies and I remain.	Du fällst – ich werde stehn.

ROCCO

My hands are cold and trembling.	Die Glieder fühl' ich beben,
What fever wracks my brain?	Wie könnt ich das bestehn?
I will not kill this pris'ner,	Ich nehm' ihm nicht das Leben,
So come what may, that's plain.	Mag, was da will, geschehn.
To take a life, your lordship,	Nein, Herr, das Leben nehmen,
Is not my duty here.	Das ist nicht meine Pflicht.

PIZARRO

I'll see to that myself then	Ich will mich selbst bequemen,
If your own courage fails;	Wenn dir's an Mut gebricht;
Go down, delay no longer,	Nun eile rasch und munter
To him who lies below there,	Zu jenem Mann hinunter,
You know . . .	Du weisst . . .

ROCCO

. . . You mean to him	. . . Der kaum mehr lebt
Who lives a ling'ring death?	Und wie ein Schatten schwebt?

PIZARRO
(grimly)

To him! Go down to him,	Zu dem, zu dem hinab!
I'll wait there at a distance.	Ich wart' in kleiner Ferne,
Whilst down in that old cistern	Du gräbst in der Zisterne
You dig his grave.	Sehr schnell ein Grab.

ROCCO

And then? And then?	Und dann? Und dann?

PIZARRO

Then, hidden in my cloak,	Dann werd' ich selbst, vermummt,
I'll steal into the dungeon.	Mich in den Kerker schleichen:
One thrust . . .	Ein Stoss . . .

(he shows the dagger)

. . . and he's no more!	. . . und er verstummt!

ROCCO
(aside)

Both starved and bound in fetters,	Verhungernd in den Ketten,
For long he's known such pain,	Ertrug er lange Pein,
That knife will surely save him,	Ihn töten, heisst ihn retten,
And set him free again.	Der Dolch wird ihn befrei'n.

PIZARRO
(aside)

He'll die where he lies fettered,	Er sterb' in seinen Ketten,
Too short was all his pain,	Zu kurz war seine Pein!
Until he's dead and buried,	Sein Tod nur kann mich retten,
My peace I'll never gain.	Dann werd' ich ruhig sein.

Now, Rocco, this matter's urgent!	Jetzt, Alter, jetzt hat es Eile!
Do you understand me?	Hast du mich verstanden?
You'll give a signal	Du gibst ein Zeichen!
Then, hidden in my cloak	Dann werd ich selbst, vermummt,

I'll steal into the dungeon.	Mich in den Kerker schleichen;
One thrust and he's no more!	Ein Stoss – und er verstummt!

ROCCO

Both starved and bound in fetters	Verhungernd in den Ketten
For long he's known such pain,	Ertrug er lange Pein,
The knife would surely save him,	Ihn töten, heisst ihn retten,
And set him free again.	Der Dolch wird ihn befrei'n.

PIZARRO

He dies where he lies fettered,	Er sterb' in seinen Ketten,
Too short was all his pain,	Zu kurz war seine Pein!
Until he's dead and buried	Sein Tod nur kann mich retten,
My peace I'll never gain.	Dann werd' ich ruhig sein.

Exit to garden. Rocco follows him. **Scene Six.** /*Recitative and Aria No. 9*

LEONORA
(in a state of violent emotion)

Perfidious wretch! Where do you haste?	Abscheulicher! Wo eilst du hin?
What evil plan now stirs within you?	Was hast du vor in wildem Grimme?
Compassion's voice, or human feelings	Des Mitleids Ruf, der Menschheit Stimme,
Can nothing move your tiger's heart?	Rührt nichts mehr deinen Tigersinn?
Yet though the storm of anger rages	Doch toben auch wie Meereswogen
Deep in that savage breast of yours,	Dir in der Seele Zorn und Wut,
For me a distant rainbow shimmers,	So leuchtet mir ein Farbenbogen,
Serene against the stormy flood.	Der hell auf dunklen Wolken ruht:
It brings me peace, my fears are banished,	Der blickt so still, so friedlich nieder,
It wakens memories long vanished,	Der spiegelt alte Zeiten wieder,
And calmer flows my fevered blood.	Und neu besänftigt wallt mein Blut.
Sweet hope, oh never let your star, [16]	Komm, Hoffnung, lass den letzten Stern
Your last faint star of comfort be denied me.	Der Müden nicht erbleichen!
Oh come, shine forth and light my path, tho'it be long and far,	Erhell mein Ziel, sei's noch so fern,
For love will surely guide me.	Die Liebe wird's erreichen.
Some inner voice now calls me.	Ich folg' dem innern Triebe,
I'll show no fear,	Ich wanke nicht,
My path lies here,	Mich stärkt die Pflicht
My faithful heart shall guide me.	Der treuen Gattenliebe!
Oh you for whom I've borne the past,	O du, für den ich alles trug,
Could I but come to find you.	Konnt' ich zur Stelle dringen,
Where savage hate still chains you fast,	Wo Bosheit dich in Fesseln schlug,
Some word of hope to bring you!	Und süssen Trost dir bringen!
Some inner voice now calls me.	Ich folg' dem innern Triebe,
I'll show no fear,	Ich wanke nicht,
My path lies here,	Mich stärkt die Pflicht
My faithful heart shall guide me.	Der treuen Gattenliebe!

Exit to garden. **Scene Seven.** *Marcellina comes out of the house. Jacquino follows her.*

JACQUINO

But Marcellina . . .	Aber, Marzelline –

Not a word, not a syllable. I won't have any more of your silly sighs, and that's that.

Kein Wort, keine Silbe. Ich will nichts mehr von deinen albernen Liebesseufzern hören, und dabei bleibt es.

JACQUINO

Who could have foretold that when I decided to fall in love with you? In those days, yes, I was the good, kind Jacquino, here, there and everywhere, the one who had to put your iron on the stove, fold the linen for you, take parcels to the prisoners, in short do everything that a respectable girl could require of a respectable boy. But since this Fidelio . . .

Wer mir das vorher gesagt hätte, als ich mir vornahm, mich recht ordentlich in dich zu verlieben. Damals, ja da war ich der gute, der liebe Jaquino an allen Orten and Ecken. Ich musste dir das Eisen in den Ofen legen, Wäsche in Falten schlagen, Päckchen zu den Gefangenen bringen, kurz alles tun, was ein ehrbares Mädchen einem ehrbaren Junggesellen erlauben kann. Aber seit dieser Fidelio –

MARCELLINA
(quickly breaking in)

I won't deny that I was fond of you, but look, I'll be honest with you, that wasn't love. Fidelio attracts me much more, and between him and me I feel a much greater understanding.

Ich leugne nicht, ich war dir gut, aber sieh, ich bin offenherzig, das war keine Liebe. Fidelio zieht mich weit mehr an, zwischen ihm and mir fühle ich eine weit grössere Übereinstimmung.

JACQUINO

What? Understanding with some vagrant boy from God knows where, who your father found at the gate and took in out of sheer pity, who . . . who . . .

Was? Übereinstimmung mit einem solchen hergelaufenen Jungen, der Gott weiss woher ist, den der Vater aus blossem Mitleid am Tor dort aufgenommen hat, der – der –

MARCELLINA
(irritably)

Who's poor and abandoned . . . and who I'm going to marry.

Der arm and verlassen ist – und den ich doch heirate.

JACQUINO

D'you think I'm going to allow that? To stop that happening under my eyes, watch out that I don't cause trouble!

Glaubst du, dass ich das leiden werde? He, däss es ja nicht in meiner Gegenwart geschieht, ich möchte euch einen gewaltigen Streich spielen!

Scene Eight. *The same. Rocco, Leonora come from the garden.*

ROCCO

What are you two quarrelling about?

Was habt ihr denn beide wieder zu zanken?

MARCELLINA

Oh father, he's always nagging at me.

Ach, Vater, er verfolgt mich immer.

ROCCO

Why's that?

Warum denn?

MARCELLINA

He wants me to love him, says I've got to marry him.

Er will, dass ich ihn lieben, dass ich ihn heiraten soll.

JACQUINO

Yes, yes, she must love me, must at least

Ja, ja, sie soll mich lieben, sie soll mich

marry me, and I . . .	wenigstens heiraten, und ich –

ROCCO

What? Have I cared so well for my only daughter,	Was? Ich sollte eine einzige Tochter so gut gepflegt

(patting Marcellina on the cheek)

gone to so much trouble raising her 'til she's sixteen, all that for the gentleman there?	mit so viel Mühe bis in ihr sechzehntes Jahr erzogen haben, und das alles für den Herrn da?

(looking laughingly at Jacquino)

No Jacquino, marriage with you is out of the question; my mind is occupied with other, more propitious prospects.	Nein, Jaquino, von deiner Heirat ist jetzt keine Rede, mich beschäftigen andere, klügere Absichten.

MARCELLINA

I understand, father.	Ich verstehe, Vater.

(tenderly and softly)

Fidelio!	Fidelio!

LEONORA

Enough of that for now. Rocco, you know I've asked you before to allow the poor prisoners who live at ground level out into the castle garden. You've always promised but then put it off. Today the weather is so fine, and the Governor doesn't come here at this time.	Brechen wir davon ab. – Rocco, ich ersuchte Euch schon einige Male, die armen Gefangenen, die hier über der Erde wohnen, in unsern Festungsgarten zu lassen. Ihr verspracht und verschobt es immer. Heute ist das Wetter so schön, der Gouverneur kommt um diese Zeit nicht hierher.

MARCELLINA

Oh yes, I agree with him.	O ja! Ich bitte mit ihm!

ROCCO

Children, without the Governor's permission?	Kinder, ohne Erlaubnis des Gouverneurs?

MARCELLINA

He spoke with you for such a long time. Perhaps he had some special request for you, and so he won't be so strict.	Aber er sprach so lange mit Euch. Vielleicht sollt Ihr ihm einen Gefallen tun, und dann wird er es so genau nicht nehmen.

ROCCO

A special request? You're right Marcellina, because of that I can risk it. Right then, Jacquino and Fidelio, open the upper cells. Meanwhile I'll go to Pizarro and occupy him, while I	Einen Gefallen? Du hast recht, Marzelline. Auf diese Gefahr hin kann ich es wagen. Wohl denn, Jaquino and Fidelio, öffnet die leichteren Gefängnisse. Ich aber gehe zu Pizarro und halte ihn zurück, indem ich

(to Marcellina)

speak to him on your behalf.	für dein Bestes rede.

MARCELLINA
(presses his hand)

That's right, father.	So recht, Vater.

Rocco goes into the garden. Leonora and Jacquino open the heavily-secured cell doors and withdraw with Marcellina into the background to watch sympathetically as the prisoners gradually emerge. **Scene Nine.** *Finale No. 10 | During the prelude, the prisoners gradually fill the stage.*

CHORUS OF PRISONERS [17]

Oh what delight! To breathe the air,	O welche Lust! in freier Luft
The open air around us.	Den Atem leicht zu heben!
Here light still comes to greet us;	Nur hier, nur hier ist Leben,
This dungeon is a tomb.	Der Kerker eine Gruft.

A PRISONER [18]

We trust for our deliv'rance	Wir wollen mit Vertrauen
In Heaven's help and guidance,	Auf Gottes Hilfe bauen.
The voice of hope still whispers here	Die Hoffnung flüstert sanft mir zu:
We shall be freed, we shall find peace.	Wir werden frei, wir finden Ruh!

THE OTHERS

Deliv'rance! Rescue! Glorious dream!	O Himmel! Rettung! Welch' ein Glück!
Oh freedom, will you be ours once again?	O Freiheit! Kehrest du zuruck?

An officer appears on the wall and then withdraws.

SECOND PRISONER

Speak softly, guard your ev'ry word	Sprecht leise! haltet euch zuruck!
For we're both watch'd and overheard.	Wir sind belauscht mit Ohr und Blick.

CHORUS

(Speak softly) guard your ev'ry word (Have a care),	Sprecht leise, haltet euch zurück!
For we're both watch'd and overheard.	Wir sind belauscht mit Ohr und Blick.
Oh what delight! To breathe the air	Sprecht leise, ja leise!
The open air around us.	O welche Lust! In freier Luft
Here life still comes to greet us.	Den Atem leicht zu heben! O welche Lust!
	Nur hier, nur hier ist Leben.
(Speak softly) guard your ev'ry word (Have a care),	Sprecht leise, haltet euch zurück!
For we're both watch'd and overheard.	Wir sind belauscht mit Ohr und Blick.

Before the Chorus has quite finished, Rocco enters at the back of the stage and talks urgently to Leonora. The prisoners move away into the garden. Marcellina and Jacquino follow them. Rocco and Leonora come forward. **Scene Ten./**Recitative

LEONORA

Tell me, what news?	Nun sprecht, wie ging's?

ROCCO

So far, so good.	Recht gut, recht gut!
I tried to do the best I could,	Zusammen rafft' ich meinen Mut
I told him of our plans,	Und trug ihm alles vor;
And all we'd hoped for,	Und sollt'st du's glauben,
And you shall hear what he replied.	Was er zur Antwort mir gab?
Your marriage was quickly approved and from this morning,	Die Heirat und dass du mir hilfst, will er erlauben;
You'll come to help me in the dungeons by my side.	Noch heute führ ich in die Kerker dich hinab.

Duet

LEONORA

This morning? this morning?	Noch heute, noch heute?
Oh happy day, what glorious tidings.	O welch ein Glück, o welche Wonne!

ROCCO

I see that gives you pleasure,	Ich sehe deine Freude;
In just a moment now,	Nur noch ein Augenblick,
We'll both go down together.	dann gehen wir schon beide –

LEONORA

Go down, to where?   Wohin?

ROCCO

     Down to that man below,   Zu jenem Mann hinab,
For many weeks I've starved him   Dem ich seit vielen Wochen
And giv'n him less to eat each day.   Stets weniger zu essen gab.

LEONORA

Ah! Have they now reprieved him?   Ha! Wird er losgesprochen?

ROCCO

Oh no!   O nein!

LEONORA

  What then? Come say!   So sprich!

ROCCO

       Alas, no, no!   O nein!
       (mysteriously)
We'll set him free, but how? Take care . . . Wir müssen ihn, doch wie? – befrei'n.
In just an hour, no longer,   Er muss in einer Stunde –
(No word of this remember)   Den Finger auf dem Munde –
We must inter him there!   Von uns begraben sein.

LEONORA

Then he is dead?   So ist er tot?

ROCCO

     Not yet, not yet!   Noch nicht, noch nicht!

LEONORA
(recoiling)
And then to kill him, is your task? Ist ihn zu töten deine Pflicht?

ROCCO

No. My good lad, you need not fear, Nein, guter Junge, zittre nicht!
For murder's not for Rocco here.   Zum Morden dingt sich Rocco nicht.
My lord himself will be at hand;   Der Gouverneur kommt selbst hinab;
We do but dig the grave, he's planned. Wir beide graben nur das Grab.

LEONORA
(aside)
Perhaps the grave of my own husband, Vielleicht das Grab des Gatten graben?
What more frightful could there be?   O was kann fürchterlicher sein!

ROCCO

I could not give him food or water.   Ich darf ihn nicht mit Speise laben,
The grave at least will bring him peace. Ihm wird im Grabe besser sein!
No time to waste, we must get ready. [19] Wir müssen gleich zum Werke schreiten;
I'll need your help, keep calm and steady, Du musst mir helfen, mich begleiten;
Hard is the jailer's gloomy task.   Hart ist des Kerkersmeisters Brot.

LEONORA

I'll follow you, do all you ask.   Ich folge dir, wär's in den Tod.

ROCCO

The ruined well will serve our purpose In der zerfallenen Zisterne
It won't take long as you will see.   Bereiten wir die Grube leicht.
Believe me, I don't like this bus'ness Ich tu'es, glaube mir, nicht gerne

| You are too troubled, seems to me! | Auch dir ist schaurig, wie mich deucht. |

LEONORA

| I've not done work like this before. | Ich bin es nur noch nicht gewohnt. |

ROCCO

I would have spared you this, be sure,	Ich hätte gerne dich verschont,
But it's too much for me alone	Doch wird es mir allein zu schwer,
My lord's impatient to be done.	Und gar so streng ist unser Herr.

LEONORA
(aside)

| My heart will break – | O welch ein Schmerz! |

ROCCO
(aside)

| I fear he's weeping. | Mir scheint, er weint. |
(aloud)
| No, you stay here, I shall not need you. | Nein, du bleibst hier, ich geh alleine, |
| I'll go alone. | ich geh allein. |

LEONORA
(earnestly pressing herself upon him)

No, let me go,	O nein, O nein!
For I must see that pris'ner	Ich muss ihn seh'n, den Armen sehen.
(Although my life should be in danger,	Und müsst' ich selbst zu Grunde gehn!
Tho' I myself should die down there.)	

ROCCO AND LEONORA

| No more delay, what may befall | O säumen wir nun länger nicht, |
| We'll answer duty's fearful call. | Wir folgen unserer strengen Pflicht. |

Scene Eleven. *Jacquino and Marcellina hurry in breathlessly.*

MARCELLINA [20]

| Oh father dear! | Ach! Vater, eilt! |

ROCCO

| Now what is wrong? | Was hast du denn? |

JACQUINO

| Do not delay! | Nicht länger weilt! |

ROCCO

| What's gone amiss? | Was ist geschehn? |

MARCELLINA

| Pizarro's coming round this way. | Voll Zorn folgt mir Pizarro nach! |
| He's threat'ning you! | Er drohet dir! |

JACQUINO

| Do not delay! | Nicht länger weilt! |

ROCCO

| Be calm, be calm! | Gemach! gemach! |

LEONORA

| Get out of sight! | So eilet fort! |

ROCCO

| Just let me know, | Nur noch dies Wort: |
| Say has he heard? | Sprich, weiss er schon? |

JACQUINO

Yes, of course he's heard.	Ja, er weiss es schon.

MARCELLINA

Somebody said to him that we'd	Der Offizier sagt' ihm, was wir
Let all the prisoners come out of here.	Jetzt den Gefangenen gewähren.

ROCCO

Well, let them all go back at once, then!	Lasst alle schnell zurücke kehren!

Exit Jacquino to garden.

MARCELLINA

Remember how he rages,	Ihr wisst ja, wie er tobet,
You know his angry mood.	Und kennet seine Wut.

She goes after Jacquino.

LEONORA
(aside)

My heart within me rages	Wie mir's im Innern tobet!
And will not be subdued!	Emporet ist mein Blut!

ROCCO
(aside)

My conscience reassures me,	Mein Herz hat mich gelobet,
Despite the tyrant's mood.	Sei der Tyrann in Wut!

Scene Twelve. *Enter Pizarro.*

PIZARRO [21]

Presumptuous scoundrel, do you dare commit	Verwegner Alter, welche Rechte
Such an outrage as I see?	Legst du dir frevelnd selber bei?
What servant ever had permission	Und ziemt es dem gedungnen Knechte,
To let the prisoners go free?	Zu geben die Gefangenen frei?

ROCCO
(in confusion)

Good sir.	O Herr!

PIZARRO

Speak up!	Wohlan!

ROCCO
(looking for an excuse)

The sun is shining	Des Frühlings Kommen,
The Spring begins to smile again,	Das heitre warme Sonnenlicht,
And . . .	Dann . . .

(composing himself)

. . . Have you realised what further	. . . Habt ihr wohl in Acht genommen,
Speaks in my favour here today?	Was sonst zu meinem Vorteil spricht?

(taking his cap off)

Our Sov'reign's name-day, we are keeping,	Des Königs Namensfest ist heute,
We honour him like this each year.	Das feiern wir auf solche Art.

(quietly to Pizarro)

Death waits below, so let these others here,	Der unten stirbt – doch lasst die andern
Take the air a moment longer.	Jetzt fröhlich hin und wieder wandern;
Let all your anger fall on him.	Fur *jenen* sei der Zorn gespart!

PIZARRO
(softly)

Go dig his grave, your task is urgent,	So eile, ihm sein Grab zu graben,
Here I will have both peace and quiet.	Hier will ich stille Ruhe haben.
Back to their cells with all these men.	Schliess die Gefangenen wieder ein,
Never dare disobey again.	Mögst du nie mehr verwegen sein!

THE PRISONERS
(coming back from the garden) [22]

Farewell to spring and heaven's light,	Leb wohl, du warmes Sonnenlicht,
Joys all too soon denied us.	Schnell schwindest du uns wieder!
Once more the gloom will hide us,	Schon sinkt die Nacht hernieder,
Our days are but eternal night.	Aus der so bald kein Morgen bricht.

MARCELLINA
(watching the prisoners)

We led them forth to heaven's light,	Wie eilten sie zum Sonnenlicht,
And now they all must leave us.	Und scheiden traurig wieder!

(aside)

Here danger hovers round us	Die Andern murmeln nieder,
And joy gives way to cheerless night.	Hier wohnt die Lust, die Freude nicht!

LEONORA
(to the prisoners)

No more delay, you heard aright	Ihr hört das Wort, drum zögert nicht,
Go back into your dungeons!	Kehrt in den Kerker wieder!

(aside)

Where can we look for justice	Angst rinnt durch meine Glieder.
To shame this tyrant in men's sight?	Ereilt den Frevler kein Gericht?

JACQUINO
(to the prisoners)

No more delay, you heard aright,	Ihr hört das Wort, drum zögert nicht,
Go back into your dungeons.	Kehrt in den Kerker wieder.

(aside, watching Rocco and Leonora)

They're plotting something serious,	Sie sinnen auf und nieder!
I'd like to know what it's about!	Könnt' ich verstehn, was jeder spricht!

PIZARRO

Now Rocco, quick get out of sight	Nun, Rocco, zögre länger nicht,
You know what lies before us!	Steig in den Kerker nieder.

(softly)

You must not dare come back here,	Nicht eher kehrst du wieder,
Stay down there, until I've put this wrong to right.	Bis ich vollzogen das Gericht.

ROCCO

My lord, I'll work with all my might,	Nein, Herr, ich zögre länger nicht,
Yes, I'll obey your orders.	Ich steige eilend nieder.

(aside)

Hard is the task before us,	Mir beben meine Glieder;
My limbs are cold and numb with fright.	O unglückselig harte Pflicht!

The prisoners return to their cells, which Leonora and Jacquino lock behind them.

Engraving of the Second Act of 'Fidelio' by V.R. Grüner, from the 'Wiener Hoftheater-Taschenbuch' of 1815. (National Library, Vienna) Below: the same scene in the ENO production with Neil Howlett (Pizarro), Josephine Barstow (Leonora) and Alberto Remedios (Florestan) (photo: Andrew March)

Act Two

A dark subterranean dungeon. Left, a well covered with stones and rubble. In the background are several openings in the wall, covered by grilles, through which a flight of steps leading upwards is visible. On the right is the last step and the door to the cell. A lamp is burning.

Scene One. *Florestan sits on a stone, his body chained by a long fetter to the wall. | Orchestral prelude and Aria No. 11*

FLORESTAN [23]

God! What endless night! What grim, foreboding silence!

Naught stirs within these walls. Naught lives down here but me.

How harsh this trial! Yet Thy will, oh God, is righteous.

I'll not complain. What I must suffer, [24] lies with Thee.

In the Spring of life's young morning [25]
All my joy departed!
Words of truth I bravely uttered,
And these chains are my reward.
I will bear my grief with patience
Die in shame when my course has run.
Yet my heart can still find solace,
For my duty I have done.

(in rapture, bordering on delirium) [26]

What gentle soft breezes around me now play?

What brightens my grave with such splendour?

I see there an angel in roseate array,

Her glances are gentle and tender . . .

An angel who resembles Leonora, the wife whom I love,

Who leads me to freedom in heaven above.

Gott! welch' Dunkel hier! O grauenvolle Stille.

Od' ist es um mich her: nichts lebet ausser mir.

O schwere Prüfung! – Doch gerecht ist Gottes Wille!

Ich murre nicht! Das Mass der Leiden steht bei dir.

In des Lebens Frühlingstagen
Ist das Glück von mir geflohn!
Wahrheit wagt' ich kühn zu sagen,
Und die Ketten sind mein Lohn.
Willig duld' ich alle Schmerzen,
Ende schmählich meine Bahn;
Süsser Trost in meinem Herzen:
Meine Pflicht hab' ich getan!

Und spür' ich nicht linde, sanft säuselnde Luft?

Und ist nicht mein Grab mir erhellet?

Ich seh', wie ein Engel im rosigen Duft

Sich tröstend zur Seite mir stellet,

Ein Engel, Leonoren, der Gattin, so gleich,

Der führt mich zur Freiheit ins himmlische Reich.

He drops, exhausted, on the boulder, covering his face in his hands.

Scene Two. *Rocco and Leonora are seen climbing down the steps by the light of a lantern, carrying a jug and digging tools for the grave. The door at the back opens, and the stage is partly lit. | Melodrama and Duet No. 12*

Melodrama
LEONORA
(sotto voce)

How cold it is in this underground vault.

Wie kalt ist es in diesem unterirdischen Gewölbe!

ROCCO

Of course it is – it's so deep.

Das ist natürlich, es ist ja so tief.

LEONORA
(glancing uneasily around)

I thought we'd never even find the entrance.

Ich glaubte schon, wir würden den Eingang gar nicht finden.

ROCCO
(hurrying towards Florestan)

There he is.   Da ist er.

LEONORA
(haltingly, trying to recognise the prisoner)

He doesn't even seem to move . . .   Er scheint ganz ohne Bewegung.

ROCCO

Perhaps he's dead.   Vielleicht ist er tot.

LEONORA
(shuddering)

D'you think so?   Ihr meint es?

Florestan moves.

ROCCO

No, no he's asleep. We must take   Nein, nein, er schläft. – Das müssen wir
advantage of that. There's no time to lose.   benutzen und gleich ans Werk gehen; wir
                                 haben keine Zeit zu verlieren.

LEONORA
(aside)

I can't see his face. God stand by me if it   Es ist unmöglich, seine Züge zu
is him.   unterscheiden. – Gott steh' mir bei,
                                 wenn er es ist!

ROCCO
(puts his lamp down on the rubble)

Here, under this rubble, is the cistern I   Hier, unter diesen Trümmern ist die
told you about. We won't need to dig   Zisterne, von der ich dir gesagt habe. –
much to find the opening. Give me a   Wir brauchen nicht viel zu graben, um
pick-axe, and stand there.   an die Öffnung zu kommen. Gib mir
                                 eine Haue, und du, stelle dich hierher.

He climbs into the hole up to his waist, sets down the jug and places his bunch of keys beside him. Leonora stands on the edge and hands him the pick.

You're trembling. Are you afraid?   Du zitterst, fürchtest du dich?

LEONORA
(speaking firmly)

No, it's just that it's so cold.   O nein, es ist nur so kalt.

ROCCO
(briskly)

Get on with it then, the work will warm   So mache fort, im Arbeiten wird dir
 you up.   schon warm werden.

As the duet begins, Rocco starts digging; when he bends down Leonora watches the prisoner. The duet is sung sotto voce throughout. / Duet [27]

ROCCO
(under his breath, as he works)

We must be quick, don't waste a   Nur hurtig fort, nur frisch gegraben,
 moment.
My lord himself will soon be here.   Es währt nicht lang, er kommt herein.

LEONORA
(also working)

You'll have no reason for complaining   Ihr sollt ja nicht zu klagen haben,
I'll do my best, so have no fear.   Ihr sollt gewiss zufrieden sein.

71

ROCCO
(jacking up a large stone)

Come on. Let's see if we can shift it.	Komm, hilf doch diesen Stein mir heben!
Take care. Take care. It's no light weight.	Hab Acht! Hab Acht! Er hat Gewicht.

LEONORA
(helping to lift it)

I'll take this end, keep it straight,	Ich helfe schon, sorgt Euch nicht;
I'll hold it fast so you can lift it.	Ich will mir alle Mühe geben.

ROCCO

A fraction more!	Ein wenig noch!

LEONORA

Hold on!	Geduld!

ROCCO

It's moved!	Er weicht!

LEONORA

We'll make quite sure!	Nur etwas noch!
It's free at last.	

ROCCO

It's no light weight!	Er ist nicht leicht!

They let the stone roll over the rubble while they catch their breath.

ROCCO
(returning to work)

We must be quick, don't waste a moment,	Nur hurtig fort, nur frisch gegraben,
My lord himself will soon be here.	Es währt nicht lang, er kommt herein.

LEONORA
(also beginning to work again)

Let me but gather strength I beg you.	Lasst mich nur wieder Kräfte haben,
We'll soon be done, the end is near.	Wir werden bald zu Ende sein.

(trying to watch the prisoner; aside)

Who you may be, I'm here to save you,	Wer du auch seist, ich will dich retten,
I vow you shall not perish here!	Bei Gott, du sollst kein Opfer sein!
No more shall cruel chains enslave you,	Gewiss, ich löse deine Ketten,
You shall be rescued, that I swear.	Ich will, du Armer, dich befrei'n.

ROCCO
(suddenly straightening up)

Why this delay, what's this I see?	Was zauderst du in deiner Pflicht?

LEONORA
(setting to work again)

No, father, no, I'll not delay, come bear with me.	Nein, Vater, nein, ich zaudre nicht.

ROCCO

Come waste no more time, take care,	Nur hurtig fort, nur frisch gegraben,
My lord himself will soon be here.	Es währt nicht lang, so kommt er her.

LEONORA

You'll have no reason for complaining.	Ihr sollt ja nicht zu klagen haben,
Let me but gather strength, I beg you.	Lasst mich nur wieder Kräfte haben,
No work will be too hard for me	Denn mir wird keine Arbeit schwer.
Father, I'll not fail you, have no fear!	

Rocco drinks. Florestan comes round and raises his head without turning towards Leonora.

LEONORA

He's waking!   Er erwacht!

ROCCO

(suddenly stopping drinking)

Waking, is he?   Er erwacht, sagst du?

LEONORA

(in great confusion, looking at Florestan)

Yes, he's just raised his head.   Ja, er hat eben den Kopf in die Höhe
                                                    gehoben.

ROCCO

No doubt he'll start asking all those   Ohne Zweifel wird er wieder tausend
questions again. I must speak with him   Fragen an mich stellen. Ich muss allein
at once. He'll soon be dead.   mit ihm reden. Nun hat er es bald
                                                    überstanden.

He climbs out of the grave.

You get down there instead and clear as   Steig du statt meiner hinab und räume
much away as we need to find the   noch so viel weg, dass man die Zisterne
opening to the cistern.   öffnen kann.

LEONORA

(goes down a few steps, shivering)

There are no words for what is going   Was in mir vorgeht, ist unaussprechlich!
through my mind.

ROCCO

(pauses slightly, then to Florestan)

Well, have you rested a little?   Nun, Ihr habt wieder einige Augenblicke
                                                    geruht?

FLORESTAN

Rested? How could I find rest?   Geruht? Wie fände ich Ruhe?

LEONORA
(aside)

That voice! If only I could see his face,   Diese Stimme! – Wenn ich nur einen
just for an instant.   Augenblick sein Gesicht sehen könnte.

FLORESTAN

Will you always be deaf to my pleas, you   Werdet Ihr immer bei meinen Klagen
heartless man?   taub sein, grausamer Mann?

(looking towards Leonora as he speaks the last words)

LEONORA
(aside)

God! It is him.   Gott! Er ist's!

She falls unconscious on the edge of the grave.

ROCCO

What do you want of me? I carry out the   Was verlangt Ihr denn von mir? Ich
orders I get. That is my job and my   vollziehe die Befehle, die man mir gibt;
duty.   das ist mein Amt, meine Pflicht.

FLORESTAN

Tell me at least, who is the Governor of   Sagt mir endlich einmal, wer ist
this prison?   Gouverneur dieses Gefängnisses?

ROCCO
(aside)

It can't do any harm now.

Jetzt kann ich ihm ja ohne Gefahr genugtun.

(to Florestan)

The Governor of this prison is Don Pizarro.

Der Gouverneur diese Gefängnisses ist Don Pizarro.

FLORESTAN

Pizarro!

Pizarro!

LEONORA

(recovering gradually)

Monster! Your cruelty restores my strength.

O Barbar! Deine Grausamkeit gibt mir meine Kräfte wieder.

FLORESTAN

Send as soon as possible to Seville, ask for Leonora Florestan . . .

O schickt so bald als möglich nach Sevilla, fragt nach Leonore Florestan –

LEONORA

Dear God! He has no idea that even now she is digging his grave!

Gott! Er ahnt nicht, dass sie jetzt sein Grab gräbt!

FLORESTAN

Let her know that I am lying here in chains.

Sagt ihr, dass ich hier in Ketten liege.

ROCCO

That's not possible, I tell you. I'd destroy myself without having helped you.

Es ist unmöglich, sag ich Euch. Ich würde mich ins Verderben stürzen, ohne Euch genützt zu haben.

FLORESTAN

Then if I'm fated to end my life here, at least don't let me waste slowly away.

Wenn ich denn verdammt bin, hier mein Leben zu enden, o so lasst mich nicht langsam verschmachten.

LEONORA

(jumping up and leaning against the wall)

Oh God, how am I to bear this?

O Gott! Wer kann das ertragen?

FLORESTAN

Out of pity give me a little water. That's not asking much.

Aus Barmherzigkeit, gib mir nur einen Tropfen Wasser. Das ist ja so wenig.

ROCCO

(aside)

Against my will I'm touched.

Es geht mir wider meinen Willen zu Herzen.

LEONORA

He seems to be giving in.

Er scheint sich zu erweichen.

FLORESTAN

You give me no answer?

Du gibst mir keine Antwort?

ROCCO

I can't get you what you ask for. All I

Ich kann Euch nicht verschaffen, was Ihr

| can give you is what's left of some wine in my jug. Fidelio! | verlangt. Alles, was ich Euch anbieten kann, ist ein Restchen Wein, das ich in meinem Kruge habe. – Fidelio! |

LEONORA
(quickly bringing the jug)

| Here it is, here it is! | Da ist er! Da ist er! |

FLORESTAN
(looking at Leonora)

| Who is that? | Wer ist das? |

ROCCO

| My turnkey and soon to be my son-in-law. | Mein Schliesser und in wenigen Tagen mein Eidam. |

(gives Florestan the jug)

| Drink. It's only a little wine but I give it you gladly. | Trinkt! Es ist freilich nur wenig Wein, aber ich gebe ihn Euch gern. |

(to Leonora)

| You, why, you seem strangely moved? | Du bist ja ganz in Bewegung? |

LEONORA
(confused)

| Who wouldn't be? You too, Master Rocco . . . | Wer sollte es nicht sein? Ihr selbst, Meister Rocco – |

ROCCO

| It's true. The man has such a voice . . . | Es ist wahr, der Mensch hat so eine Stimme . . . |

LEONORA

| Yes. It strikes to the very depth of the soul. | Jawohl, sie dringt in die Tiefe des Herzens. |

Trio No. 13

FLORESTAN [28]

| Some better world, one day, reward you, Kind heaven has guided you here, My thanks, your help to me is dear, Though for your kindness I cannot recompense you. | Euch werde Lohn in bessern Welten, Der Himmel hat euch mir geschickt. O Dank! Ihr habt mich süss erquickt; Ich kann die Wohltat nicht vergelten. |

ROCCO
(softly to Leonora, whom he draws to his side)

| I gladly help one such as he, He's not much longer left to live. | Ich labt' ihn gern, den armen Mann, Es ist ja bald um ihn getan. |

LEONORA
(aside)

| My heart is racing past belief! It beats with joy and bitter grief. | Wie heftig pocht dieses Herz! Es wogt in Freud' und scharfem Schmerz! |

FLORESTAN
(aside)

| The lad seems moved I'm bound to say. The man himself was kind to me. | Bewegt seh' ich den Jüngling hier, Und Rührung zeigt auch dieser Mann, |

Oh God, you send me hope today　　　　O Gott, du sendest Hoffnung mir,
That I may win their loyalty.　　　　　Dass ich sie noch gewinnen kann.

LEONORA
(aside)

The fearful hour at last is near,　　　　Die hehre, bange Stunde winkt,
That brings me death or rescue here.　　Die Tod mir oder Rettung bringt.

ROCCO
(aside)

My duty thus commanded me,　　　　　Ich tu', was meine Pflicht gebeut,
Tho' I still hate such cruelty.　　　　　Doch hass' ich alle Grausamkeit.

LEONORA
(softly to Rocco, taking a piece of bread from the satchel)
This piece of bread, that I have with me,　Dies Stückchen Brot, ja seit zwei Tagen
I've kept it here since yesterday.　　　　Trag' ich es immer schon bei mir.

ROCCO

A kindly thought, I'm bound to say,　　Ich möchte gern, doch sag' ich dir,
But now we simply dare not risk it.　　　Das hiesse wirklich zu viel wagen.

LEONORA
(coaxing him)
Yet,　　　　　　　　　　　　　　Ach!
You freely gave him wine just now.　　Ihr labtet gern den armen Mann.

ROCCO

But here's a thing I can't allow.　　　Das geht nicht an, das geht nicht an.

LEONORA
(as before)

He's not much longer left to live!　　Es ist ja bald um ihn getan!

ROCCO

All right then, yes all right, well you　So sei es, ja, du kannst es wagen!
    may risk it.

LEONORA
(with deep emotion, giving the bread to Florestan)
Come take this bread, unhappy man.　Da nimm das Brot, du armer Mann!

FLORESTAN
(grasping Leonora's hand and pressing it to him)
My grateful thanks, my thanks, my　　O, Dank dir, Dank! O Dank!
    thanks!
May some better world one day reward　Euch werde Lohn in bessern Welten,
    you
For heav'n itself has sent you here.　　Der Himmel hat euch mir geschickt.
My thanks! Your help to me is dear.　　O Dank! Ihr habt mich süss erquickt.
Such kindness I cannot repay.

LEONORA

May heaven send you rescue here　　Der Himmel schicke Rettung dir,
For then will my reward be near.　　　Dann wird mir hoher Lohn gewährt.
You gave him comfort here just now,
Poor, lonely, man!

Though deeply moved by all your grief	Mich rührte oft dein Leiden hier,
To help you, I was not allowed.	Doch Hilfe war mir streng verwehrt.

(aside)

I'm glad to comfort such as he,	Ich labt' ihn gern, den armen Mann,
The end is near as you can see,	Es ist ja bald um ihn getan.
Soon death will come to seek him here!	
Unhappy, lonely man!	

LEONORA

Oh this is more than I can bear!	O mehr, als ich ertragen kann!

FLORESTAN

For such good deeds could I reward you!	O dass ich Euch nicht lohnen kann!

Florestan eats the bread.

ROCCO

(to Leonora, after a moment's silence)

Everything's ready. I'll give the signal.	Alles ist bereit. Ich gehe, das Signal zu geben.

(going to the back of the stage)

LEONORA

Oh God, give me strength and courage.	O Gott, gib mir Mut und Stärke!

FLORESTAN

(to Leonora, as Rocco goes to open the doors)

Where is he going?	Wo geht er hin?

Rocco opens the doors and gives the signal with a sharp whistle.

Is that the harbinger of my death?	Ist das der Vorbote meines Todes?

LEONORA

(deeply moved)

No, no! Be calm, dear prisoner!	Nein, nein! Beruhige dich, lieber Gefangener.

FLORESTAN

My Leonora . . . am I then never to see you again?	O meine Leonore! So soll ich dich nie wieder sehen?

LEONORA

(drawn to Florestan but attempting to master the impulse)

How my heart draws me to him!	Mein ganzes Herz reisst mich zu ihm hin!

(to Florestan)

Be calm, I say. Don't forget, whatever you may see or hear, that a divine providence watches over all of us! Yes, there *is* a divine providence.	Sei ruhig, sag ich dir! Vergiss nicht, was du auch hören und sehen magst, dass überall eine Vorsehung ist. – Ja, ja, es gibt eine Vorsehung!

Leonora moves away towards the well. **Scene Three.** *The same. Pizarro, muffled in a cloak.*

PIZARRO

(to Rocco, disguising his voice)

Everything ready?	Ist alles bereit?

ROCCO

Yes, we only need to open the cistern.	Ja, die Zisterne braucht nur geöffnet zu werden.

<table>
<tr><td colspan="2" align="center">**PIZARRO**</td></tr>
<tr><td>Good. Get rid of the boy.</td><td>Gut, der Junge soll sich entfernen.</td></tr>
</table>

<table>
<tr><td colspan="2" align="center">**ROCCO**</td></tr>
<tr><td colspan="2" align="center">*(to Leonora)*</td></tr>
<tr><td>Go. Be off.</td><td>Geh, entferne dich!</td></tr>
</table>

<table>
<tr><td colspan="2" align="center">**LEONORA**</td></tr>
<tr><td colspan="2" align="center">*(very confused)*</td></tr>
<tr><td>Who? Me? But you . . .</td><td>Wer? – Ich? – Und Ihr?</td></tr>
</table>

<table>
<tr><td colspan="2" align="center">**ROCCO**</td></tr>
<tr><td>Haven't I still to take the prisoner's
chains off? Go, go!</td><td>Muss ich nicht dem Gefangenen die
Eisen abnehmen? Geh, geh!</td></tr>
</table>

Leonora goes to the back of the stage and gradually approaches Florestan in the shadows, keeping her eyes on Pizarro.

<table>
<tr><td colspan="2" align="center">**PIZARRO**</td></tr>
<tr><td colspan="2" align="center">*(aside, glancing at Rocco and Leonora)*</td></tr>
<tr><td>I must dispose of these two today to
make sure that everything's kept under
cover.</td><td>Die muss ich mir noch heute beide vom
Halse schaffen, damit alles verborgen
bleibt.</td></tr>
</table>

<table>
<tr><td colspan="2" align="center">**ROCCO**</td></tr>
<tr><td colspan="2" align="center">*(to Pizarro)*</td></tr>
<tr><td>Shall I take off his fetters?</td><td>Soll ich ihm die Ketten abnehmen?</td></tr>
</table>

<table>
<tr><td colspan="2" align="center">**PIZARRO**</td></tr>
<tr><td>No. Just free him from the stone.</td><td>Nein, aber schliesse ihn von dem Stein los.</td></tr>
<tr><td colspan="2" align="center">*(aside)*</td></tr>
<tr><td>Time presses.</td><td>Die Zeit ist dringend.</td></tr>
</table>

He draws a dagger. | Quartet No. 14

<table>
<tr><td colspan="2" align="center">**PIZARRO**</td></tr>
<tr><td>It's time now. Yes, but first I'll tell him
Whose blade shall pierce his righteous
   heart.
No more I'll hide my secret from him,
Look here! I was not tricked by you!</td><td>Er sterbe! Doch er soll erst wissen,
Wer ihm sein stolzes Herz zerfleischt.

Der Rache Dunkel sei zerrissen,
Sieh her! Du hast mich nicht getäuscht!</td></tr>
<tr><td colspan="2" align="center">*(he throws off his cloak)*</td></tr>
<tr><td>Pizarro, whom you would have ruined.
Pizarro, whom you should have dreaded,
Now claims his vengeance here!</td><td>[29] Pizarro, den du stürzen wolltest,
Pizarro, den du fürchten solltest,
Steht nun als Rächer hier.</td></tr>
</table>

<table>
<tr><td colspan="2" align="center">**FLORESTAN**</td></tr>
<tr><td colspan="2" align="center">*(calmly)*</td></tr>
<tr><td>A murd'rer, here I see.</td><td>Ein Mörder steht vor mir!</td></tr>
</table>

<table>
<tr><td colspan="2" align="center">**PIZARRO**</td></tr>
<tr><td>Once more let me recall
The wrong you've done to me.
And so without delay
This blade of mine . . .</td><td>Noch einmal ruf' ich dir,
Was du getan, zurück;
Nur noch ein Augenblick,
Und dieser Dolch –</td></tr>
</table>

He is about to stab Florestan. Leonora hurls herself forward with a piercing cry and shields Florestan with her body.

<table>
<tr><td colspan="2" align="center">**LEONORA**</td></tr>
<tr><td align="center">Stand back!</td><td align="right">Zurück!</td></tr>
</table>

<table>
<tr><td colspan="2" align="center">**FLORESTAN**</td></tr>
<tr><td>Oh God!</td><td>O Gott!</td></tr>
</table>

ROCCO

What's this?   Was soll?

LEONORA

Your dagger   Durchbohren

Must pierce my own heart first.   Musst du erst diese Brust.
May death soon be your sentence   Der Tod sei dir geschworen
For all your evil crimes.   Für deine Mörderlust.

PIZARRO
(pushing her away)

       You maniac!   Wahnsinniger!

ROCCO
(to Leonora)

       Stand back!   Halt ein!

PIZARRO

I'll make you pay for this.   Er soll bestrafet sein!

LEONORA
(once more shielding her husband)

First, kill his wife!   [30] Töt' erst sein Weib!

ROCCO AND PIZARRO

His wife?   Sein Weib?

FLORESTAN

My wife!   Mein Weib!

LEONORA
(to Florestan)

Yes, I am Leonora!   Ja, sieh hier Leonoren!

FLORESTAN

Leonora!   Leonore!

LEONORA
(to the others)

I am his wife, I swore   Ich bin sein Weib, geschworen
I would rescue him and ruin you.   Hab' ich ihm Trost, Verderben dir!

PIZARRO
(aside)

What an audacious deed!   Welch' unerhörter Mut!

FLORESTAN
(to Leonora)

My heart beats high with joy.   Vor Freude starrt mein Blut!

ROCCO
(aside)

My blood runs cold with fear.   Mir starrt vor Angst mein Blut!

LEONORA
(aside)

His anger I defy, yes!   Ich trotze seiner Wut!

PIZARRO

Must I give way before a woman?   Soll ich vor einem Weibe beben?

79

LEONORA

May death soon be your sentence!   Der Tod sei dir geschworen!

PIZARRO

My victims both of them shall be!   So opfr' ich beide meinem Grimm.
He rushes at Leonora and Florestan.

LEONORA

Your dagger must pierce my own heart   Durchbohren musst du erst diese Brust!
first.

PIZARRO

You shared your life with that poor   Geteilt hast du mit ihm das Leben,
  madman,
So die with him and share his fate!   So teile nun den Tod mit ihm.

LEONORA
(quickly pointing a pistol at him)
Say but a word and you shall die!   Noch einen Laut – und du bist tot!
The sound of the trumpet call from the tower is heard. [31, 32]

LEONORA
(embracing Florestan)
Ah! That brings salvation! God be   Ach, du bist gerettet! Grosser Gott!
praised!

FLORESTAN

Ah! That brings salvation! God be   Ach, ich bin gerettet! Grosser Gott!
praised!

PIZARRO
(stunned)
Ah! Don Fernando! Cursed fate!   Ha, der Minister! Höll' und Tod!

ROCCO
(stunned)
Ah! What's this I hear? Oh, righteous   O was ist das, gerechter Gott!
God!

The trumpet sounds again, louder.[31]

Scene Four. *The same. Jacquino. Soldiers appear with torches at the uppermost grille on the staircase.*

JACQUINO
(speaking)
Father Rocco! The Minister is arriving,   Vater Rocco! Der Herr Minister kommt
his party's at the gate!   an. Sein Gefolge ist schon vor dem
     Schlosstor.

ROCCO
(aside, startled and happily)
God be praised!   Gelobt sei Gott!
(very loudly to Jacquino)
We're coming, yes we're coming straight-   Wir kommen – ja, wir kommen
away. Men with torches, summon them   augenblicklich. Und diese Leute mit
to accompany the Governor up!   Fackeln sollen heruntersteigen und den
     Herrn Gouverneur hinaufbegleiten.
The soldiers come down to the door. Exit Jacquino.

LEONORA AND FLORESTAN

The hour of retribution!   Es schlägt der Rache Stunde!

(Your) (My) danger now is past.	(Du) (Ich) sollst gerettet sein!
(For) (Your) courage and devotion	Die Liebe wird im Bunde
Will set (you) (me) free at last.	Mit Mute (dich) (mich) befrein!

PIZARRO

They mock me in derision,	Verflucht sei diese Stunde!
This hour shall be accursed.	Die Heuchler spotten mein;
Despairing frenzy drives me,	Verzweiflung wird im Bunde
I'll have revenge at last.	Mit meiner Rache sein.

ROCCO

I'm lost in this confusion,	O fürchterliche Stunde!
What now will come to pass?	O Gott, was wartet mein?
No longer will I serve him	Ich will nicht mehr im Bunde
The tyrant stands unmasked.	Mit diesem Wütrich sein.

Pizarro rushes out. Rocco gives Leonora a reassuring gesture as he leaves. Soldiers with torches precede them. **Scene Five.** *Leonora. Florestan.*

FLORESTAN

My Leonora! Dearest wife! Angel miraculously sent by God to save me, come to my heart!	Meine Leonore! Geliebtes Weib! Engel, den Gott wie ein Wunder zu meiner Rettung mir gesendet, lass an dies Herz dich drücken.

(embracing her)

Can we still hope?	Aber dürfen wir noch hoffen?

LEONORA

We can. The arrival of the Minister, whom we know, Pizarro's confusion and, above all, Father Rocco's consoling gestures are grounds enough for me to believe that our sufferings are at an end and the hour of good fortune is at hand.	Wir dürfen es. Die Ankunft des Ministers, den wir kennen, Pizarros Verwirrung und vor allem Vater Roccos tröstende Zeichen sind mir ebenso viele Gründe, zu glauben, unser Leiden sei am Ziele und die Zeit unseres Glückes wolle beginnen.

FLORESTAN

Tell me, how did you come here?	Sprich, wie kamst du hierher?

LEONORA
(quickly)

I left Seville, came on foot and in man's clothes, the gaoler took me into his service, and your persecutor himself made me his turnkey.	Ich verliess Sevilla, ich kam zu fuss in Manneskleidern, der Kerkermeister nahm mich in seine Dienste, dein Verfolger selbst machte mich zum Schliesser.

FLORESTAN

Faithful wife! Woman without equal! What have you suffered on my account?	Treues Weib! Frau ohnegleichen! Was hast du meinetwegen erduldet?

LEONORA

Nothing, my Florestan! I was with you in spirit; how could my body not have been strong when it was fighting for its better self?	Nichts, mein Florestan! Meine Seele war mit dir; wie hätte der Körper sich nicht stark gefühlt, indem er für sein besseres Selbst kämpfte?

LEONORA

Oh sweet delight beyond all telling!	O namenlose Freude!
By my dear husband's side.	Mein Mann an meiner Brust!

FLORESTAN

O sweet delight beyond all telling!	O namenlose Freude!
By Leonora's side.	An Leonorens Brust!

BOTH

Our grief is now forgotten	Nach unnennbarem Leide
And joy returns at last.	So übergrosse Lust!

LEONORA

With you once more I stand united!	Du wieder nun in meinen Armen!

FLORESTAN

Kind heav'n at last our faith requited.	O Gott! Wie gross ist dein Erbarmen!

BOTH

Give thanks to God, our friend and guide,	O Dank dir, Gott für diese Lust!
My love, my life is at my side.	Mein (Mann), mein (Mann) an meiner Brust! (Weib) (Weib)

FLORESTAN

My life!	Du bist's!

LEONORA

My love!	Ich bin's!

FLORESTAN

What heav'n descended pleasure!	O himmlisches Entzücken!
Leonora!	Leonore!

LEONORA

Florestan!	Florestan!

BOTH

Oh sweeet delight beyond all telling,	O namenlose Freude!
Our grief is now forgotten	Nach unnennbarem Leide
And joy returns at last.	So übergrosse Lust!
(My love, my life) to me restored (My wife, my wife)	
Thanks be to God for this reward.	

Scene Six. *The same. Rocco.*

ROCCO
(bursting in)

Good news, you poor suffering creatures! His Excellency the Minister has brought a list of all the prisoners with him, and all of them are to be presented to him. Jacquino is already opening the upper cells.	Gute Botschaft, ihr armen Leidenden! Der Herr Minister hat eine Liste aller Gefangenen mit sich; alle sollen ihm vorgeführt werden. Jacquino öffnet die oberen Gefängnisse.

(to Florestan)

You alone are not mentioned on the list. Your imprisonment here was a personal act on the part of the Governor. Come,	Ihr allein seid nicht erwähnt. Euer Aufenthalt hier ist eine Eigenmächtigkeit des Gouverneurs. Kommt, folgt mir hin-

follow me. And you,too, dear lady! And if God grants power to my words, and if he rewards the heroic action of this most noble wife, then you will be set free, and your good fortune is the result of my efforts!

auf. Auch Ihr, gnädige Frau. Und gibt Gott meinen Worten Kraft und lohnt er die Heldentat der edelsten Gattin, so werdet Ihr frei, und Euer Glück ist mein Werk.

FLORESTAN

Leonora!

Leonora!

LEONORA

By what miracle!

Durch welche Wunder!

ROCCO

Come, don't delay! Up above you will learn everything. And keep those fetters on; God grant that they act as a plea for mercy, and will be put instead on the monster who caused you such suffering.

Fort, zögert nicht! Oben werdet ihr alles erfahren. Auch diese Fesseln behaltet noch. Gott gebe, dass sie Euch Mitleid erflehen und dem Grausamen angelegt werden, der Euch so viele Leiden bereitet.

Exeunt.

Scene change:*The parade ground of the castle, with a statue of the king.*

Scene Seven. *The castle guard march in and form an open square. Then from one side enters the Minister, Don Fernando, accompanied by Pizarro and officers. A crowd surges forward. From the other side, Jacquino and Marcellina lead in the state prisoners, who kneel before Don Fernando. | Finale No. 16*

CHORUS
(of Prisoners and People)

Hail glorious day, day of deliv'rance,
So long desired, so long denied,
Here clemency unites with justice,
Before the gates that guard our tomb
The gloomy gates now opened wide!

Heil sei dem Tag, Heil sei der Stunde,
Die lang ersehnt, doch unvermeint,
Gerechtigkeit mit Huld im Bunde
Vor unseres Grabes Tor erscheint!

FERNANDO [34]

Our sov'reign liege, the King, has charged me
To seek out those who've suffered here.
That I may lift this veil of evil
Shrouding you all in gloom and fear.
No! No longer kneel like slaves before me,

Des besten Königs Wink und Wille
Führt mich zu euch, ihr Armen, her,
Dass ich der Frevel Nacht enthülle,
Die All' umfangen schwarz und schwer.
Nein, nicht länger knieet sklavisch nieder,

The prisoners stand up.

No tyrant here you'll find in me.
A brother comes to seek his brothers,
If he can help, he gladly will.

Tyrannenstrenge sei mir fern!
Es sucht der Bruder seine Brüder,
Und kann er helfen, hilft er gern.

CHORUS

Hail glorious day! Day of deliv'rance.

Heil sei dem Tag, Heil sei der Stunde!

FERNANDO

A brother comes to seek his brothers,
If he can help, he gladly will.

Es sucht der Bruder seine Brüder,
Und kann er helfen, hilft er gern.

Scene Eight. *Rocco pushes his way through the guard, followed by Leonora and Florestan.*

ROCCO

My lord then show this pair your mercy.

Wohlan, so helfet! Helft den Armen!

PIZARRO

What's this I see? Ha!   Was seh' ich? Ha!

ROCCO
(to Pizarro)

This moves you then?   Bewegt es dich?

PIZARRO
(to Rocco)

Go back!   Fort, fort!

FERNANDO
(to Rocco)

Continue!   Nein rede!

ROCCO

Oh, have pity,   All' Erbarmen,
These two poor suff'rers need your aid.   Vereine diesem Paare sich!

Florestan comes forward.

Don Florestan . . .   Don Florestan . . .

FERNANDO
(amazed)

I thought he'd perished,   Der Totgeglaubte,
That noble soul who fought for truth?   Der Edle, der für Wahrheit stritt?

ROCCO

For that he suffered endless grief.   Und Qualen ohne Zahl erlitt.

FERNANDO

The friend, the friend, I thought had   Mein Freund! Mein Freund! Der
    perished?   Totgeglaubte?
In fetters, pale and wracked with pain.   Gefesselt, bleich steht er vor mir.

ROCCO AND LEONORA

Yes, Florestan returns again.   Ja, Florestan, ihr seht ihn hier.

ROCCO
(Leonora comes forward)

And Leonora . . .   Und Leonore . . .

FERNANDO
(still more astonished)

Leonora?   Leonore!

ROCCO

The pearl of women, here you see,   Der Frauen Zierde führ' ich vor;
She came to me . . .   Sie kam hierher –

PIZARRO

My lord, one moment.   Zwei Worte sagen . . .

FERNANDO

Stand back!   *Kein* Wort!
(to Rocco)

She came?   Sie kam –

ROCCO

. . . Here to my door . . .	. . .dort an mein Tor
Dressed as a youth she joined my service,	Und trat als Knecht in meine Dienste
Working so well, that I decided	Und tat so brave, treue Dienste,
She'd be my future son-in-law.	Dass ich zum Eidam sie erkor.

MARCELLINA

What tidings! Heavens! What is this I hear?	O weh mir, was vernimmt mein Ohr!

ROCCO

Pizarro at this very hour,	Der Unmensch wollt' in dieser Stunde
Had come down to put this man to death!	Vollziehn an Florestan den Mord.

PIZARRO
(in the utmost rage)

With *their* connivance!	Vollziehn, *mit* ihm! –

ROCCO
(indicating himself and Leonora)

Yes, *our* connivance!	Mit *uns* im Bunde!

(to Fernando)

But your arrival stayed his hand.	Nur euer Kommen rief ihn fort.

CHORUS
(with great animation)

This tyrant here shall pay for this,	Bestrafet sei der Bösewicht,
Let justice wield her sword,	Der Unschuld unterdrückt.
For all these harsh and cruel deeds,	Gerechtigkeit hält zum Gericht
He'll reap a just reward.	Der Rache Schwert Gezückt.

At a sign from Fernando, Pizarro is taken away.

FERNANDO
(to Rocco)

You opened up his grave today,	Du schlossest auf des Edlen Grab,
Now go and take his chains away.	Jetzt nimm ihm seine Ketten ab –
No, wait. You, you his noble wife,	Doch halt! Euch, edle Frau, allein,
Yes, you alone shall set him free.	Euch ziemt es ganz ihn zu befrein.

LEONORA
(taking the key, she releases Florestan with great emotion from his fetters; he falls into her arms)

Oh God! Oh what happiness!	[35] O Gott! – Welch' ein Augenblick!

FLORESTAN

Oh joy that words could not express!	O unaussprechlich süsses Glück!

FERNANDO

Your judgement, Lord, is right and just, withal.	Gerecht, O Gott, ist dein Gericht!

MARCELLINA AND ROCCO

You try us, yet you guard us all.	Du prüfest, du verlässt uns nicht.

ALL

Oh God! What blessed happiness!	O Gott! welch' ein Augenblick!
Oh joy that words could not express!	O unaussprechlich süsses Glück!
Your judgement, Lord, is just withal.	Gerecht, O Gott, ist dein Gericht,
You try us, yet you guard us all!	Du prüfest, du verlässt uns nicht!

Let all join in our rejoicing
For the prize of such a wife,
Ne'er can this be praised too highly
Thus to save a husband's life.

Wer ein holdes Weib errungen,
Stimm'in unsern Jubel ein!
Nie wird es zu hoch besungen,
Retterin des Gatten sein.

FLORESTAN

By your love I was protected,
Faith and virtue triumph here!

Deine Treu' erhielt mein Leben,
Tugend schreckt den Bösewicht.

LEONORA

Love alone my path directed,
True devotion knows no fear!

Liebe führte mein Bestreben,
Wahre Liebe fürchtet nicht.

CHORUS

Praise her courage and acclaim
Leonora's noble name!

Preist mit hoher Freude Glut
Leonorens edlen Mut!

FLORESTAN
(stepping forward and indicating Leonora)

Let all join in our rejoicing
For the prize of such a wife,
Ne'er can this be praised too highly
Thus to save a husband's life.

Wer ein solches Weib errungen,
Stimm' in unsern Jubel ein!
Nie wird es zu hoch besungen,
Retterin des Gatten sein.

LEONORA
(embracing him)

Love alone released you from your
      bondage,
Love has broken ev'ry chain,
Joyful hearts sing out your message,
Florestan is mine again.

Liebend ist er mir gelungen,

Dich aus Ketten zu befrein.
Liebend sei es hoch besungen,
Florestan ist wieder mein!

CHORUS

Let all join in our rejoicing
For the prize of such a wife,
Ne'er can this be praised too highly,
Thus to save a husband's life.

Wer ein holdes Weib errungen
Stimm' in unsern Jubel ein!
Nie wird es zu hoch besungen,
Rettern des Gatten sein.

LEONORA

Love released you from your bondage,
Florestan returns to life.

Liebend sei es hoch besungen:
Florestan ist wieder mein!

ALL THE OTHERS

Ne'er can this be praised too highly
Thus to save her husband's life.

Nie wird es zu hoch besungen,
Retterin des Gatten sein.

THE END

The final scene in the ENO production by Joachim Herz, designed by Reinhart Zimmermann, with costumes by Eleonore Kleber (photo: Andrew March).

A fresco by Moritz von Schwind from the Vienna State Opera showing a scene from 'Fidelio'. (reproduced by permission of the Trustees of the British Museum)

Bibliography

A very selective list from the many books about Beethoven available in English.

The biography of Beethoven by Thayer, an American whose work was published in the last century (in German) remains the basic text about the composer's life; this is now available in English (edited and revised by Elliot Forbes, Princeton 1970). The account of Beethoven left by his pupil, Schindler, *(Beethoven as I knew him*, edited by MacArdle, translated by C S Jolly, London 1966) is invaluable, if prejudiced. The essay by Grove (London, 1951) on Beethoven is illuminating. Almost all of Beethoven's letters were translated by Emily Anderson (3 vols., London 1961) and a selection, edited by Alan Tyson, is available *(Selected Letters of Beethoven*, Macmillan, 1967). *Beethoven: A Documentary Study*, compiled by H Robbins London (Thames & Hudson, 1970) contains beautiful illustrations and a vast number of translated documents written by Beethoven's contemporaries.

Discography   In order of UK release. All performances are in stereo unless asterisked* and in German.

Conductor Company/Chorus	*Fricsay* **Bavarian State** **Opera**	*Klemperer* **Philharmonia** **Orch. & Chorus**	*Maazel* **VPO/Vienna** **State Opera** **Chorus**
Don Fernando	K. Engen	F. Crass	H. Prey
Don Pizarro	D. Fisher-Dieskau	W. Berry	T. Krause
Florestan	E. Haefliger	J. Vickers	J. McCracken
Leonore	L. Rysanek	C. Ludwig	B. Nilsson
Rocco	G. Frick	G. Frick	K. Böhme
Marzelline	I. Seefried	I. Hallstein	G. Sciutti
Jacquino	F. Lenz	G. Unger	D. Grobe
1st Prisoner	—	K. Wehofshitz	K. Equiluz
2nd Prisoner	—	R. Wolansky	G. Adam
Disc UK number	DG 2705-073	SLS 5006	SET 272-3
Tape UK number	—	TC-SLS 5006	—
Excerpts (Disc)	—	—	SXL 6276
Excerpts (Tape)	—	—	—
Disc US number	—	3-Ang S-3625	2-Lon 1259
Tape US Number	—	—	—
—			

Karajan **Berlin PO/ German Opera Chorus**	*Böhm* **Dresden State OP. Orch & Chorus**	Bernstein **VPO/Vienna State Opera Chorus**	Blomstedt **Dresden Staats- kapelle/Leipzig Radio Chorus**
J. van Dam	M. Talvela	D. Fischer-Dieskau	H.-C. Polster
Z. Keleman	T. Adam	H. Sotin	T. Adam
J. Vickers	J. King	R. Kollo	R. Cassilly
H. Dernesch	G. Jones	G. Janowitz	E. Moser
K. Ridderbusch	F. Crass	M. Jungwirth	K. Ridderbusch
H. Donath	E. Mathis	L. Popp	H. Donath
H. Laubenthal	P. Schreier	A. Dallapozza	E. Buchner
W. Hollweg	E. Buchner	A. Sramek	—
S. Rudolf	G. Leib	K. Terkal	—
SLS 954	2721 136	2709 082	SLS 999
—	3378 054	3371 039	—
—	—	2537 048	—
—	—	3305 048	—
3-Ang S-3773	3-DG 2709031	3-DG 2709082	—
—	—	3371 039	—

The essay by Lord Harewood in *Opera on Record* (edited by Alan Blyth, Hutchinson, 1979) vividly introduces us to the many interpretations on record.

Excerpts

Number	Artists	UK Numbers only Disc Number ✶✶ Tape
O wär ich schon	P. Lorengar	SXL6525
Mir ist so wunderbar	Robson/Jones/Kelly/Dobson	
	Covent Garden/Solti	SET 392 - 3
Ha! Welch ein' Augenblick	G. Evans	SXL6262
Abscheulicher	B. Nilsson	SXL6077
Excerpts (arr. Sedlak)	London Wind Soloists/	
	Brymer	SDD 485